CALCUTTA PAST AND PRESENT

CALCUTTA PAST AND PRESENT

KATHLEEN BLECHYNDEN

GYAN

Published by

Gyan Publishing House
5, Ansari Road
Daryaganj, New Delhi-110002
Phone: 011-47034999, 9811692060
E-mail: books@gyanbooks.com

Distribution Network
gyanbooks.com
India, USA, Canada, UK, Australia

ISBN: 978-93-7225-160-9 (HB)

First Published, 1905

2nd Impression 2025

Printed at: Gyan Press, Delhi.

CALCUTTA PAST AND PRESENT
Author: KATHLEEN BLECHYNDEN

CALCUTTA: PAST AND PRESENT

General View of CALCUTTA, taken near the Sluice of Fort William.

From an engraving by W. Baillie, 1794.

CALCUTTA PAST AND PRESENT

By KATHLEEN BLECHYNDEN

1905

PREFACE

In a field of research which has known the learned labours of Sir Henry Yule, Mr. J. Talboys Wheeler, the Record Commission, and Mr. H. Beveridge, followed by Dr. Busteed, the Rev. H. B. Hyde, and the late Mr. C. R. Wilson, it might have been thought that there was little room for other workers; yet, where the harvest is so abundant, a simple gleaner may venture to follow in the wake of these stalwart reapers, and bring her modest sheaf to the great storehouse of history.

Such a thought has encouraged me to put forward this little book. My aim has not been to give any account of the great deeds by which the men of old Calcutta laid the foundations of the British Empire in the East, but rather to try and depict the lives they led, their daily cares and amusements, the wives and daughters who lightened their exile, the houses in which they dwelt, the servants who waited on them, the food they ate, the wines they drank, the scenes amid which they moved, the graves in which they laid their loved ones or sank themselves to rest.

In gathering material for these pages I have had the great advantage of a family connection with Calcutta, extending over many years, which has placed at my disposal old diaries and other personal records, besides maps of the town on which changes and improvements were recorded as they were made. These, together with an intimate knowledge of the city, gained during several years' residence in it, have enabled me to construct a mental picture of the life of old Calcutta, which is so vivid as to leave an impression of having really borne a part in it myself. It is this picture, this sense of reality, which I have tried—inadequate as I feel the effort has been—to convey to my readers.

For the illustrations I am greatly indebted to the publishers, who have spared neither trouble nor expense in reproducing old portraits and engravings, as well as modern photographs. They will be found to be, some of them unique, and all, we believe, of great interest, and such as are not readily available to the larger number of those who are interested in the subject.

In conclusion, I may say that, wherever I have taken information or quoted from the published writings of others, I have been careful to acknowledge my authority. And if the book as a whole owes its inspiration to the labours of others, it is so in every department of human effort; for each fresh toiler must ever hear, echoing out of the past, the message that came to Kipling's builder from the wreckage of a former builder's plan, "Tell him, I too, have known."

K. B.

1905.

CONTENTS

CHAPTER I

EARLY YEARS

CHAPTER II

THE SIEGE AND CAPTURE

CHAPTER III

RECOVERY AND AFTER

CONTENTS

CONTENTS

CHAPTER VIII

TOLD BY THE TOMBS

CHAPTER IX

STREETS AND HOUSES

CHAPTER X

NEAR AND FAR

LIST OF ILLUSTRATIONS

LIST OF ILLUSTRATIONS

LIST OF ILLUSTRATIONS

CALCULTTA
PAST AND PRESENT

CHAPTER I

EARLY YEARS

Founding of Calcutta by Charnock in 1690—The three villages and their situation—Charnock's grave and its opening in 1892—The 1715 embassy to Delhi—Surgeon Hamilton, his services, death, and epitaph—The building of the old fort—The church—The park—Social conditions.

A DAY in August in the height of the rainy season in Bengal. The muddy waters of the Hughly, beaten level by the ceaseless downpour of the rain descending in heavy unbroken rush, heaved sullenly in thick turbid swell, rising higher and ever higher as the strong downward current was met and checked by the force of the rising tide, rushing in from the distant sea. In the great circling whirlpools formed by the opposing forces, the bloated carcases of drowned animals, great branches of trees, or whole trees with a tangled mass of roots, swept round, lashed by the rain and whirling flood into semblance of some living monster, stretching octopus-like arms. Once and again would sweep by a human form, charred from the funeral pyre, borne on the rushing waters of the sacred stream to meet its final dissolution, devoured by the alligators, vultures, crows, and jackals who haunted the river waves and shores in watchful eagerness for their prey.

Moving carefully and slowly up stream with the rising tide, came a varied fleet of merchant vessels, and small "country boats," which had ridden together at the last safe anchorage, and now toilsomely accomplished another stage of their journey on the dangerous waterway. Sailing with the others came a little "country ship," commanded by an English seaman, Captain Brooke, and bearing a small company of Englishmen, servants of the Honourable Company of East India merchants. Their destination was the village of Chuttanutty, where they had traded at various intervals for several years past. Steering for "the great tree" which was the "sea mark," the worthy captain brought his vessel to a safe anchorage in the deep water below the high bank on which the village stood; and this is how the record of the arrival stands in the old books of the company:—

"1690. August 24th. This day, at Sankraal, ordered Captain Brooke to come up with his vessel to Chuttanutty, where we arrived about noon, but found the place in a deplorable condition, nothing being left for our present accommodation, and the rain falling day and night. We are forced to betake ourselves to boats, which, considering the season of the year, is very unhealthy, Mullick Burcoodar and the country people, at our leaving this place, burning and carrying away what they could."

In this way was Calcutta founded, and such was the manner of the coming of Job Charnock to his last port—the spot where his bones were to lie beneath a stately mausoleum through the centuries, while the settlement he founded amid every circumstance of discouragement and discomfort grew and prospered till it became the capital city of the British Empire in India, such an Empire as the wildest dreams of the Great Mogul never compassed.

Before proceeding further, we may well pause and try to conjure up the three villages, set amid marsh and forest, which at that time occupied the site on which Calcutta now stands. Chuttanutty, where Charnock landed, was a thriving village occupied by weavers, and, by reason of its position on the river-bank at a part where deep water afforded safe anchorage to the trading vessels passing up and down the great waterway, it commanded a good trade in cotton cloths and thread. The name Chuttanutty, or *Sutanuti*—derived from *suta*, thread, and *nuti*, a hank—has been fancifully translated Cottonopolis. The site of Chuttanutty is now occupied by the northern portion of the town: the river-bank at this point has changed less than has been the case lower down, so that Hatkola, as nearly as can be judged, covers the position of the village, and Dharmatola or Mohunton's Ghat that of Chuttanutty Ghat, the actual spot on which Charnock and his companions must have landed.

Lying somewhat back from the river, to the south of Chuttanutty, was Calcutta, occupying the highest ground in the neighbourhood now covered by the business quarter of the town, and extending down Bow Bazar. The southern boundary of this village was a creek or *khal*, which, coming from the marshy ground to the east, made its way to the river by a course which may, roughly, be said to be now marked by Hastings Street. Various derivations, learned and fanciful, have been suggested for the name "Calcutta," a large number based on a supposed connection with the Kalighat Temple. This derivation has been conclusively shown to be impossible, "philologically, as well as from a Hindu religious point of view," by a learned Hindu writer, but there seems no apparent reason why the name may not have originated from the position of the village on the bank of the *Khal*, *Khal-Kutta*, where the creek or stream had cut its way in some great flood, or had been cut by the villagers to drain their low-lying fields.

The third village, Govindpore, was like Chuttanutty, situated on the river-bank, but considerably lower down. The site is occupied by Fort William. All round this village, extending from the Calcutta *Khal* ("the Creek") to the Govindpore *Nullah* (Tolly's Nullah), covering the whole of the *maidan* of the present day, spread a jungle tract of heavy undergrowth and giant trees, the remains of a once dense forest of Soondrie trees, similar to, and possibly a portion of, the forests which give their name to the Soonderbunds or Soondrie forests of the Gangetic Delta. This *jungle* was intersected by numerous creeks and watercourses, where the muddy yellow waters of the Hughly swept in with the rising tide, or ebbed with the drainage of the surrounding rain-drenched country. A desolate tract, it was haunted by wild beasts, and by armed bands of robbers more to be dreaded than they. These made their headquarters in the village of Govindpore, dashing out in swift little boats to attack and plunder rich cargo-boats as they lay at anchor on the fog-bound river in the dark nights of the rainy and cold seasons, or, turning inland, to fall on and rob footsore and wayworn pilgrims as they toiled on the last stage of their pilgrimage to the shrine of Kali at Kalighat.

The pilgrim route, which here passed through the jungle, is clearly traceable, from the point at Chitpore, where it enters the boundary of modern Calcutta, along Chitpore Road, through Bentinck Street, and so by Chowringhee and Bhowanipore to Kalighat. In Bentinck Street, between Waterloo Street and British India Street, the road crossed "the Creek," and from there, till it reached Bhowanipore, it was called Chowringhee's Road, after Jungal Gir Chowringhee, a pious worshipper of Kali's great consort Shiva. Jungal Gir Chowringhee was the founder of a sect who were known by his name, and who worshipped at a small and very ancient temple of Shiva which stood on the bank of the Govindpore Nullah (Tolly's Nullah) a little above the Zeerut Bridge. This temple was afterwards deserted, and, falling into ruins, was long a decaying landmark in that part of the town, remaining till late into the nineteenth century. Chowringhee doubtless kept the pilgrim road through the jungle in repair as a pious duty, and the grateful pilgrims knew it by his name, which in later years became synonymous with rank and fashion in the English city.

After the English settled in Calcutta, and as year by year the villages grew and spread, the Govindpore jungle was steadily cleared away as brushwood was cut and trees felled for firewood to supply the needs of the growing population. Then came the sudden expansion of the town which followed Clive's victory at Plassey; and, the old fort having been found inadequate for the defence of the settlement, it was decided to build the new Fort William on the ground occupied by the Govindpore village, surrounded as it was by waste lands which formed a natural esplanade. In 1757 the village was removed, the inhabitants were given lands in the town and outskirts on which to build, and were paid compensation for their houses and huts destroyed. The remains of the jungle were cleared away, the land was drained, and the Calcutta *maidan* was formed, to grow in after years into a beautiful park, the pride and adornment of a beautiful city.

Such were the three villages and their surroundings when Charnock took up his residence in their midst with his half-dozen fellow-factors and guard of thirty soldiers. It may be well to recall that the Company's earlier factory had been established in Hughly, but, in 1686, owing to various causes, the English traders had come to an open rupture with the Mohammedan Governor, and had been driven away and their property confiscated. Great confusion followed, and for five years there was a constant succession of friendly overtures from one side or the other, continually thwarted by personal prejudice or violence, or by belated orders from England on the one hand and Dacca on the other, inducing fresh friction and renewing disputes which had been arranged in the interval. During the continuance of this comedy of errors, Charnock, who was the Company's principal agent in Bengal, had twice stayed at Chuttanutty while conducting negotiations with the Hughly authorities. On the second occasion, he had stayed for the best part of a year, and had erected some buildings: it is to these the entry in the diary already quoted alludes as having been "burned or carried away, nothing being left for our present accommodation."

In spite of adverse conditions, the English set themselves to work in earnest, and the minutes of the first meeting of the "Bengal

Council" at Chuttanutty are almost pathetic in the assumption of authority and observance of forms, when the surrounding circumstances are remembered. The Right Worshipful Agent Charnock, Mr. Francis Ellis, and Mr. Jeremiah Peachie duly resolved, "in consideration that all the former buildings here are destroyed," to build "as cheap as possible," a warehouse, a dining-room, a cook-room, a room to sort cloth in, an apartment for the Company's servants, and a guard-house, also a house for Mr. Ellis. The agent's and Mr. Peachie's houses, which were part standing, to be repaired, as also the secretary's office: "these to be done with mud walls and thatched, till we can get ground whereon to build a factory." These mud-walled and thatched houses, which could have been no better than native huts, were the nucleus of the city of Calcutta.

The cessation of trade during the five years' dispute with the English had made it clear to the Mohammedan rulers that a persistence in their high-handed treatment of the traders inflicted loss on themselves. There had been a change of Governors too, and under these more favourable circumstances the factory was built, and prospered. Governor Charnock, however, worn by thirty-six years of hard work and considerable suffering in Bengal, broke down: his mind gave way, and, retaining as he did his position and authority in the settlement, he brought its affairs into a state of confusion and disorder which might have proved fatal but that he died on the 10th of January, 1692, and was buried in the burial-ground of the settlement, adjoining the Creek. This burial-ground now forms St. John's Churchyard, where the mausoleum erected over Charnock's remains by his son-in-law Eyre stands to this day in excellent preservation, the lettering of its inscription almost as sharp and clear as when first raised.

Charnock's domestic history has long been the romance of the early days of Calcutta. The story runs that he saw one day a youthful Hindu widow, a girl of fifteen, about to commit *sati*, to be burnt on her husband's funeral pyre. Moved by her youth and beauty, Charnock with his bodyguard of soldiers dispersed the attendant priests and relatives, and carried away the girl, to be for twenty-five years his faithful companion through all his trials. The old records show that many of the English factors in Bengal were married to native women, many of whom became converts to the Roman Catholic faith. It is quite probable that Charnock was married to the Hindu lady, who was the mother of his daughters, three of

THE CHARNOCK MAUSOLEUM.

[*Face p.* 10.

whom married Englishmen. The eldest, Mary, was the wife of Charles Eyre, by whom the Charnock mausoleum was erected. She died four years after her father, while her husband was agent at Calcutta, and her epitaph is inscribed below that of her father, both being in Latin. It has not been ascertained where Charnock's Hindu wife died, nor the date of her death, but it has always been popularly believed that she died some years before Charnock, and that he buried her at Chuttanutty, and was himself laid in the same grave, on which, tradition says, he had yearly sacrificed a cock on the anniversary of his wife's death.

In November, 1892, two hundred years after the death of Job Charnock, the mausoleum was repaired by the Public Works Department, when advantage was taken of the opportunity to ascertain whether it contained a vault. The Rev. H. B. Hyde, at that time chaplain of St. John's, in a note read at a meeting of the Asiatic Society of Bengal in February, 1893, after stating that no trace of a vault was found, describes the result of the investigation as follows:—

"On visiting the mausoleum next morning, the 22nd of November, I found that the grave had been opened to a depth of fully six feet, at which depth the diggers had stopped, having met with a trace of human remains. The excavation was somewhat smaller than an ordinary grave, and lay east and west in the centre of the floor. At the bottom of it the workmen had cleared a level, at the western end of which they were beginning to dig a little deeper when a bone became visible. This bone was left *in situ* undisturbed, and the digging had ceased on its discovery. On seeing this bone, I felt sure it could be no other than one of the bones of the left fore-arm of the person buried, which must have lain crossed upon the breast. A little beyond it I observed a small object in the earth, which I took at first for a large coffin nail, but, on this being handed up to me, it was very apparent that it was the largest joint of, probably, a middle finger, and that, judging from its relative position, of the left hand. This bone I replaced. . . . It was quite evident that a few more strokes of the spade would discover the rest of the skeleton, perhaps perfect, after just two hundred years of burial. There can be no reasonable doubt, arguing from the position of the body and the depth at which it lay, that it was the very one to enshrine which only the mausoleum was originally built—the mortal part of the Father of Calcutta himself. Having seen what I did, I had the grave filled in . . . if the investigation were to be prosecuted at all, it should at least be in presence of a representative company of Englishmen.

For my own part, with the bones of the famous pioneer's hand accidentally discovered before me, and the strange and solemn statement of his epitaph just above them, that he had laid his mortal remains there himself *ut in spe beatæ resurrectionis ad Christi Judicis adventum obdormirent*, I felt strongly restrained from examining them further."

This opening of Charnock's grave and the uncovering of his bones proves nothing either for or against the tradition that he was laid in his wife's grave: nor does it affect the theory, held by some writers, that the ground now forming St. John's Churchyard was the first plot of land owned by the English in Calcutta, having been used by them as a burial-ground for those of their number who died while journeying up or down the river between Hughly and Balasore from 1640 onwards.

After Charnock's death Calcutta, or Chuttanutty, by which name the settlement continued to be known, grew rapidly, and within the first ten years of its existence was favoured by two fortunate circumstances which materially helped to strengthen the English position. The first was a Hindu rebellion against the Mohammedan rule, which broke out in Burdwan and Hughly and surrounding districts, and continued for two years. The foreign merchants in Bengal, viz. the English at Chuttanutty, the French at Chandernagore, and the Dutch at Chinsurah petitioned the nawab, the emperor's viceroy in Bengal, for permission to erect defensive works round their settlements as a protection against the insurgents. Receiving a careless assent in an order to defend themselves, they seized the opportunity to fortify their factories in a manner which till then had been strictly forbidden. The English began building their fort in 1699, and called it Fort William in honour of their sovereign, William III.

A second fortunate circumstance, which greatly assisted the English Company, was the appointment as Nawab of Bengal of Azim-u-shan, a grandson of the Emperor Aurungzeb, an extravagant and pleasure-loving young prince. On his arrival in Bengal the East India Company gained his favour by presenting him with an offering of one thousand gold mohurs, and he thereupon granted their petition to be allowed to purchase the *zemindari*, or landowners' rights, in the three villages of Chuttanutty, Calcutta, and Govindpore.

This was a great advance for the English Company, as it raised them at once from the position of mere adventuring traders, dependent on the caprice of the reigning nawab, to an assured status as landholders paying a yearly rental of eleven hundred and ninety-five rupees to the emperor at Delhi, and receiving in return authority to collect rents and to administer justice under the Mohammedan laws within the boundaries of the three villages. Having obtained the nawab's consent, the East India Company at once proceeded to exercise their rights without waiting to receive the emperor's confirmation of their authority, which they had great difficulty in obtaining, owing to the opposition of interested officials of the nawab's Government, who influenced the court at Delhi against them. This opposition was continued for no less than sixteen years, during which time the Company continued to exercise their rights, but were constantly thwarted and hampered by oppressive orders and various exactions, growing more intolerable every year. It was at last decided that the Company should appeal direct to the emperor in person, and it was accordingly arranged that an embassy should proceed to Delhi to try and obtain the required *firman* from the emperor, which would make the Company's position secure and relieve them of most of their grievances.

Early in 1715 the embassy proceeded to Delhi. The members were Messrs. John Surman and

Edward Stephenson, both of the Company's service, and an Armenian merchant of Calcutta, Khoja Serhaud, who acted as interpreter. They carried gifts for the emperor and his court, of "curious glass ware, clock-work, brocades, and the finest manufactures of woollen cloths and silks, valued altogether at thirty thousand pounds sterling." The Emperor Farruk Syar, hearing of these rich offerings, sent out troops to meet and escort the envoys to Delhi, where they arrived on the 7th of July, 1715, after a journey from Calcutta of three months. They were received with much honour and dignity, and proceeded immediately to pay their respects to the emperor.

Writing to Calcutta to report their proceedings, the envoys gave the following account of their reception :—

"We prepared for our first present, viz. 1,001 gold mohurs, the table clock set with precious stones, the unicorn's horn, the gold escritoire, the large piece of ambergreese, the astoa and chelumgie Manilla work, and the map of the world. These with the Honourable the Governor's letter were presented, every one holding something in his hand as usual. John Surman received a vest and culgee set with precious stones, and Serhaud a vest and culgee set with precious stones likewise, amid the great pomp and state of the Kings of Hindustan. We were very well received, and on our arrival at our house we were entertained by Sallabut Khan, with dinner sufficient both for us and our people."

In spite of this favourable reception, the emperor refused to receive the Company's petition or to transact any business till such time as his marriage with a Jodhpore princess, for which arrangements were proceeding, should have been celebrated. The envoys, thus detained, were soon plunged into the intrigues of an Indian court, and involved in counter intrigues. They were obliged to remain attending on the emperor's pleasure, and doling out such of their presents as they had reserved. They spent money lavishly, too, in winning over various nobles and others to support their petition, but after weary months of waiting they seemed no nearer the attainment of their object, and might have had to return to Calcutta disappointed but that the emperor fell ill on the eve of his marriage, and the ceremony had to be postponed.

Attached to the English embassy was Surgeon William Hamilton of the Honourable East India Company's service, whose name deserves to stand high in the records of Calcutta as second only to that of Charnock the founder. When, in spite of the efforts of the court physicians, the emperor's illness continued to increase, Hamilton proffered his services, and so successful was his treatment that the royal patient was shortly restored to health.

"As a clear demonstration to the world, he washed himself, and accordingly received the congratulations of the whole court. As a reward for Mr. Hamilton's care and success, the king was pleased to give him in public, viz. a vest, a culgee set with precious stones, two diamond rings, an elephant, horse, and 5000 rupees, besides ordering at the same time all his small instruments to be made in gold, with gold buttons for his coat and waistcoat, and brushes set with jewels."

This "demonstration" of the emperor's restoration to health took place at the end of November, when the envoys had been six months in Delhi. They now presented most of the remainder of their presents, reserving only a small part for the occasion of the king's marriage, and delivered their petition, but were informed that no business could go forward till after the ceremony. At last, in December, the royal wedding was celebrated with all the splendour which "the riches of Hindustan and two months' indefatigable labour could provide, but the envoys still had many weary delays before them, and it was not until June, 1717, that they at last received the desired *firman*, and were given permission to return to Calcutta. During this long interval Hamilton had been in attendance on the emperor, and it was largely owing to his influence that the English claims received favourable consideration in spite of opposing interests. In addition, the emperor granted permission to the East India Company to purchase the zemindary rights of twenty-four villages besides the three they already held.

So highly did Farruk Syar value Surgeon Hamilton's services, that he desired to retain him permanently at court, but to this Hamilton would by no means consent, and once more the envoys had to exercise what patience remained to them, and wait till their companion could obtain permission to accompany them. After many representations, the emperor agreed to allow Hamilton to leave him, but it was on the condition that, after he had gone to England to visit his wife and children and to procure medicines which could not be obtained in India, he would return to the emperor's service. This matter being satisfactorily arranged, the embassy at last left Delhi and returned to Calcutta, but Hamilton's compact with the emperor was never to be fulfilled. Shortly after his return to Calcutta the skilful and modest surgeon died, and was laid to his rest in the sadly crowded burial-ground of the settlement.

It has been estimated that during the seventy odd years the first Calcutta burial-ground, now St. John's Churchyard, was in use—that is, from 1692 to 1766—no less than twelve thousand bodies must have been interred in that small plot of land. Under these circumstances the same ground must have been used over and over again, and monuments can only have been erected over a few of these graves. Most of the earlier monuments fell into such a ruinous condition that, in 1802, they were taken down, and such of the memorial slabs as remained in good preservation were arranged in a pavement round the Charnock mausoleum. There they remain to this day, the long and often quaint inscriptions in raised letters as clear and fresh in many cases as though newly cut. Hamilton's grave could hardly have had any monument—apparently there was only a simple headstone bearing a record of his name and services,—for, within a very few years his resting-place appears to have been lost among the crowded graves around.

More than sixty years after Hamilton's death,

when the foundations of St. John's Church were being laid, the workmen uncovered the forgotten tombstone. Warren Hastings was then in the closing years of his Government, and he thought so highly of Hamilton's services to the East India Company that he desired to have the lettering of the epitaph gilded, and that the stone should be placed in a conspicuous position in the centre niche of the east entrance to the church. By the time the church had been completed Hastings had left the country, and the stone was placed within the Charnock mausoleum, where it has remained ever since. The inscription is in both English and Persian, the former runs as follows :—

"Under this stone lyes interred the body of William Hamilton, Surgeon, who departed this life the 4th December, 1717. His memory ought to be dear to this nation for the credit he gained the English in curing Farrukseer, the present King of Indostan, of a malignant distemper, by which he made his own name famous at the court of that great Monarch, and without doubt will perpetuate his memory as well in Great Britain as all other nations in Europe."

The following translation of the Persian inscription is given by Talboys Wheeler, in his "Early Records of British India:"—

"William Hamilton, Physician, in the service of the English Company, who had accompanied the English Ambassador to the enlightened Presence, and having made his own name famous in the four quarters of the earth by the cure of the Emperor, the Asylum of the World Muhammad Farruk Siyar the victorious: and with a thousand difficulties having obtained permission from the Court which is the refuge of the universe, to return to his country: by the Divine decree, on the fourth of December, 1717, died in Calcutta, and is buried here."

This latter inscription was apparently composed by an officer of the emperor's court, who was sent to Calcutta by his royal master to obtain confirmation of the news of Hamilton's death, which Farruk Syar imagined had been fabricated to appease him on the failure of the surgeon to return.

The poor emperor himself closed his splendid career tragically enough within three years of Hamilton's death, when, dragged from his throne and blinded by his own rebellious courtiers, he "the Asylum of the World," was brutally murdered in his dungeon after two months' miserable captivity.

With a confirmation of their rights as legal owners of their settlement and the surrounding villages, the English merchants became firmly established, and their "mud-walled and thatched" houses of a quarter of a century before had made way for brick-built terraced houses, surrounded by gardens. The three villages had grown into a thriving town containing a population of some ten or twelve hundred Europeans and a hundred thousand natives. A church had been built "by the pious charity of merchants residing there, and the Christian benevolence of seafaring men whose affairs call them to trade there." This church, which in compliment to the queen was dedicated to St. Anne, stood on the site now occupied by the western end of the Bengal Secretariat Buildings, and adjoined the main gate of the Fort, which faced "the Avenue," now Dalhousie Square North. The Avenue was a raised road which ran eastward from the Fort, through the marshy lands along the line of Bow Bazar Street, and gave access to the salt-water lakes and the ghats, where boats laden with fire-wood and jungle produce landed their cargoes for the use of the growing settlement.

Captain Hamilton, a trading seaman who visited India in the early years of the eighteenth century, published in 1727 "a new account of the East Indies," in which he gave an entertaining description of Calcutta at that period, full of little bits of local scandal, and considerably coloured by a strong prejudice against the "Conscript Fathers of the Colony," as he terms them, who appear to have got the better of the worthy seaman and shrewd trader in bargaining. This gossiping chronicler tells us—

"Fort William was built an irregular tetragon of brick and mortar called *puckah*, which is a composition of brick-dust, lime, molasses, and cut hemp, and, when it comes to be dry, is as hard and tougher than firm stone or brick."

The Fort stood on the bank of the river which flowed along what is now the Strand Road. The site has been so carefully identified and marked out in recent years that but little imagination is required to reconstruct in fancy the high walls with their bastions and buttresses which enclosed the space lying between Fairlie Place and Koila Ghat Street. With the exception of the church and the hospital, all the official buildings stood within the Fort walls. The hospital, "where many go in to undergo the penance of physick, but few come out to give any account of its operation," adjoined the burial-ground where Garstin's Buildings now stand. All other public buildings, the Government House, the barracks, the factors' houses, the writers' quarters, the warehouses, and workshops, were all in the Fort; and closely packed they must have been, for the entire length was only 710 feet, and the breadth at the northern end 340 feet, widening to 485 feet at the south.

Though the Governor's official residence, which Hamilton described as the best and most regular piece of architecture he had seen in India, stood within the Fort, he had his private dwelling-house outside the walls, for the advantage, no doubt, of wider garden space and purer air than could be obtained in the hot and overcrowded area within. This house appears to have stood about where Bankshall Street now runs, and its grounds extended across Bankshall Street to "the Park," Dalhousie Square. Round this locality gather many memories of the early days of Calcutta. It has been conjectured that the walls of the Fort were at one time coloured red, and that their ruddy reflection in the waters of the tank obtained for it its native name, "Lal Diggee," the Red Tank. However this may be, the "Great Tank" was highly valued by the settlers, for, being fed by springs, it furnished a supply of pure drinking water, very desirable when the river was polluted by every form of contamination and was the receptacle for all carrion. The tank was accordingly guarded with jealous care; the surrounding space was laid out with neat gravelled walks, and planted with orange trees and ornamental shrubs, and, surrounded by a railing, was known as "the Park," where Calcutta society promenaded in the cool of the evening. It is curious to think that, after nearly two hundred years of more or less neglect, the old glories of the Park are about to be revived under Sir Andrew Fraser's scheme, and Calcutta society in the twentieth century will pace the garden walks once trodden by their predecessors of the eighteenth century.

The upkeep of the Park cost ten rupees monthly, and in the old records are various entries of payments, such as Rs. 24 for orange trees for the use of the Park, and Rs. 20 for cleaning the tank and repairing the walks. The latest entry for repairs of the tank is dated 1753, but two years later it would appear to have fallen into a shocking state of neglect, as, in May, 1755, Mr. Holwell requested the Board that he might have permission to repair and enclose the tank and prohibit the washing of people and horses therein, the latter practice making the tank at times so offensive "there is no passing either to the southward or northward."

When Captain Hamilton wrote his account there were many ladies in Calcutta. The English ladies were chiefly the wives and daughters of the senior merchants who had accompanied their relatives from England. Other factors who had been long in the country had contracted alliances with native women, many of whom became converts to Christianity, mostly to the Romish Church. These ladies appear to have been accepted in society, and their number was added to by the wives and daughters of the Armenian merchants, who formed an important section of the community. So prosperous were these Armenians that, in 1724, they built a church, which was dedicated to St. Nazareth, in compliment to the chief promoter of the building fund, Aga Nazar, and which stands to this day, the oldest church in Calcutta.

The gossipy Captain Hamilton gives a lively description of the manners and customs of this mixed society. He says:—

"Most gentlemen and ladies in Bengal live both splendidly and pleasantly, the forenoons being dedicated to business, and after dinner to rest, and in the evening to recreate themselves in chaises or palankins, in the fields or to gardens, or by water in their budgeroes, which is a convenient boat that goes swiftly with the force of oars. On the river sometimes there is the diversion of fishing or fowling, or both: and before night they make friendly visits to one another, when pride or contention do not spoil society as too often they do among the ladies, as discord and faction do among the men."

Elsewhere the worthy captain records: "The Company has also a pretty good garden that furnishes the Governor's table with herbage and fruits, and some fish-ponds to serve his kitchen with good carp, calkops and mullet. Most of the inhabitants of Calcutta that make any tolerable figure have the same advantages; and all sorts of provisions, both wild and tame, being plentiful, good, and cheap, as well as clothing, make the country very agreeable, notwithstanding the above-mentioned inconveniences that attend it."

Chief of these "inconveniences" appears to have been the unhealthiness of the situation of Calcutta, lying as it did between the river and a great salt-water lake.

"This overflows," says Hamilton, "in September and October, and then prodigious numbers of fish resort thither; but in November and December, when the floods are dissipated, those fishes are left dry, and with their putrefaction so affect the air with thick stinking vapours which the north-east winds bring with them to Fort William that they cause a yearly mortality. One year I was there, and there were reckoned in

August about twelve hundred English, and before the beginning of January there were 460 burials registered in the clerk's book of mortality."

This terrible mortality following the rainy season continued for over half a century after Hamilton wrote, and it was quite a matter of course for men as the sickly season came round to make their wills and set their affairs in order, and for the survivors at the close of the period to congratulate each other on their escape from death.

The situation of Calcutta was not only unhealthy, but was exposed to the fierce storms which sweep up from the Bay of Bengal at the close of the south-west monsoon. On the 30th of September, 1737, such a hurricane devastated the country for sixty leagues up the Ganges, and did an immense deal of damage in Calcutta. The *Gentleman's Magazine* for June, 1738, gives a quaintly worded and harrowing account of the havoc wrought when—

"an earthquake overthrew abundance of houses, and in the storm twenty thousand ships, barks, sloops, boats, canoes, etc., were cast away, a prodigious quantity of cattle of all sorts, a great many tigers, and several rhinoceroses were drowned, even a great many caymans were stifled by the furious agitation of the waters, and an innumerable quantity of birds were beaten down into the river by the storm. Two English ships of five hundred tons were thrown into a village about two hundred fathoms above the bed of the Ganges, broke to pieces, and all the people drowned pell-mell among the inhabitants and cattle."

Curiously enough, a sentence has been interpolated by successive writers when quoting this account of the storm from the *Gentleman's Magazine*, to the effect that the steeple of the English church sank into the ground without breaking. There is no such statement in the original, though no doubt the steeple was destroyed. In a despatch from Calcutta to the Court of Directors, dated January, 1749, permission is requested for the rebuilding of the church steeple "which was thrown down in the storm, the foundation of which being already laid we imagine the expense will not exceed eight thousand rupees." Whether the storm alluded to was that of twelve years earlier, or a subsequent one, is not clear, but it is evident the steeple could not have been swallowed up entire for the foundation to have remained.

CHAPTER II

THE SIEGE AND CAPTURE

The Mahratta Ditch—Aliverdi Khan, and Suraj-ud-Dowlah—The siege and capture of Calcutta—The Black Hole, and Monument—Holwell and companions at Murshedabad, and their release.

WHILE the English settlement in Bengal grew and prospered, the Mogul Empire at Delhi was waning fast. Year after year fresh troubles arose, and, torn by internal dissension and the treachery of domestic foes, ravaged and spoiled by foreign invaders, the court had lost all control over its distant provinces. Successive nawabs of Bengal kept up a nominal allegiance to Delhi, but grew constantly more independent and more despotic in their rule, till, in 1742, when the tyranny and oppression of the then reigning nawab had become intolerable, his court and army revolted, and, selecting one of their own number, Aliverdi Khan, to be their ruler, placed him on the *gadi* as Nawab of Bengal.

During this period of lawlessness the Mahratta horsemen of Central India began to invade

Orissa and Bengal, and to lay waste whole tracts of country. Terror and consternation spread through the land, and everywhere the people fled into the jungles, or gathered in the towns and larger villages in the hope of obtaining some protection by their numbers. In Calcutta the native population undertook to dig a wide ditch which cavalry could not readily cross, round the three villages which formed the town. The ditch was to extend for seven miles, forming a semi-circle round three sides of the town, the fourth side being protected by the river. It was begun in 1742, at Chitpore, and followed the line of Circular Road southward as far as Jaun Bazar Street; here it turned to the south-west, and was intended to take a line which would have crossed the Chowringhee Road at the junction of Middleton Street, and, continuing in the same direction, would have reached the river at Hastings, about where the Commissariat buildings and jetty are now situated. This latter part, however, was not completed; for by the time some four miles of the ditch had been dug the Nawab of Bengal had come to terms with the Mahrattas, who agreed to leave Bengal unmolested in return for a yearly tribute, or *chout*. The unfinished Mahratta Ditch, which obtained for many generations of Calcutta citizens the

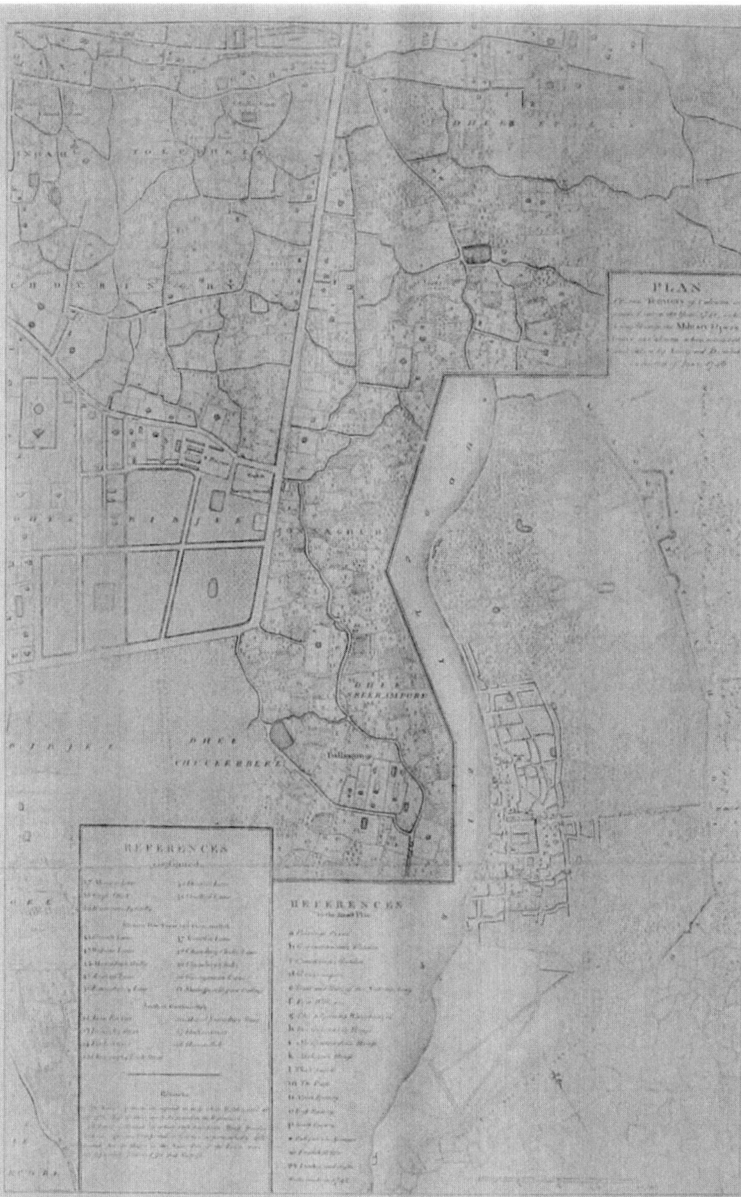

PLAN OF CALCUTTA, 1742.

SHOWING ALSO THE ROUTE OF CLIVE'S MARCH, 5TH FEBRUARY, 1757.

[Face p. 32.

soubriquet of *Ditchers*, continued as a ditch for nearly sixty years, by which time it had become a pestilential drain, unsightly and unsavoury to a degree. In 1799 it was filled up, and the Circular Road was made, which included in its width the ditch and a narrow road which had followed its course, on the town side for the entire length, and continued beyond it in a much wider sweep than the ditch had originally been intended to take. The improvement was greatly appreciated by Calcutta society of the period, and a newspaper paragraph quoted by the Rev. Mr. Long described how "in the Circular Road the young and the sprightly, in the fragrance of morning, wafted in the chariot of health, enjoy the gales of recreation."

From the time of his election as nawab in 1742, till his death in April, 1756, Aliverdi Khan ruled Bengal with strength and justice. He was succeeded by his grandson, a youth of twenty, whose name, Suraj-ud-Dowlah ("Lamp of the State") is infamous in history as the author of the terrible tragedy of the massacre of the Black Hole in Calcutta. This young man had been adopted when a child by his grandfather, the late nawab, who lavished on him a passionate tenderness which overlooked and forgave every fault. Such was the old man's infatuation, that, when the boy at the age of fifteen rebelled against him, he was distracted by fear that the lad might be wounded by his officers in defence of his authority, and himself hurried to the hostile camp, and brought the undeserving rebel home with every mark of tenderness and affection. The festivities which took place on the occasion of the double marriage of Suraj-ud-Dowlah and his younger brother, shortly after their grandfather became nawab, were "spoken of with admiration by the inhabitants of Bengal to this day," says Stewart, writing in 1813, and possibly they are still commemorated in the songs and proverbs of the country people. There were brilliant illuminations, splendid pageants, and grand processions of the two young bridegrooms. Upwards of two thousand rich dresses were distributed among the courtiers, while for a whole month the populace feasted at the expense of the nawab.

Some idea of the luxury and the high standard of living at the court of the nawabs of Bengal at Murshedabad at this period may be gathered from the following extract from the work of an anonymous Mohammedan writer, translated by Gladwin in 1788. Writing of Nawab Murshed Cooly Khan, the founder of Murshedabad, who died in 1724, the author says—

"He despised all the refinements of luxury, particularly in dress, and refrained from everything that is prohibited in the law. No high-seasoned dishes were served up to his table, neither frozen sherberts nor creams, only plain ice. During the winter Khyzir Khan, his house steward, used to collect, in the mountains of Rajmehal, a sufficient stock of ice for the rest of the year: and the whole was done at the expense of the zemindars of that district. In the mango season there was stationed at Rajmehal an overseer who used to keep a regular account of the choicest mango trees in Maldah, Kutwalee, and Husseinpoor; and his guards were placed over them to see that no one purloined the fruit, and that it was regularly sent to Murshedabad. The zemindars furnished everything that was required for these purposes, and they durst not cut down a mango tree nor touch any of the fruit that the overseer had appropriated to the use of the nawab's table."

Reared in this luxurious court, indulged to excess by his doting grandfather, flattered and fawned upon by idle and dissolute courtiers, Suraj-ud-Dowlah grew up narrow-minded, obstinate, and impatient of check or control. He appears to have had a violent dislike to the English as foreigners and interlopers, and his cupidity was roused by tales of the great wealth they were said to have amassed, and the rich spoil which might be obtained by sacking their town and factory. At the time of his accession a dispute had arisen between the English Company and the nawab, regarding a wealthy Hindu who had left Murshedabad with his family, and had settled in Calcutta under the protection of the English, who refused to surrender him to the nawab's officer. Suraj-ud-Dowlah seized the pretext to announce his intention to punish the English. His first act was to plunder the Company's factory at Cossimbazar, near Murshedabad, and to imprison the English merchants stationed there, among others being Warren Hastings, then a young writer in the company's service. Most of the prisoners were shortly released through the intercession of the French and Dutch merchants at Cossimbazar, who became bail for them, and kept them in safety until they were allowed to leave and to make their way down country to join their fellow-countrymen.

When news of the nawab's intentions reached Calcutta, the unfortunate English there were thoroughly alarmed. The long years of security had made them careless; the Fort, never very strong, had fallen into disrepair; the defences were dominated by the church, and by the private houses of the merchants, that of the

Governor in Bankshall Street, of Mr. Eyre about the middle of Fairlie Place to the north of the Fort, and of Mr. Cruttenden to the north of the church, at the junction of Lyons Range with Clive Street; while the thickly populated native town, spreading far to north and east of the Fort, was a source of serious danger. There were a very large number of Portuguese in the settlement, the degenerate descendants of the Portuguese who from very early times had tried repeatedly and unsuccessfully to establish colonies in India. These people took refuge in the Fort, and the men were armed; but, as events proved, instead of being of service, they were a terrible hindrance, and a fatal weakness in the defence. Some fifteen hundred Hindu matchlock men were also enlisted and armed, but they deserted in a body as soon as hostilities commenced.

While making such hurried preparations for defence as they could, the English continued their efforts to appease the nawab, without avail. He was bent on their destruction, and, on the 15th of June, 1756, arrived at the English outposts at Chitpore, with an army of fifty thousand men and heavy artillery, and began the assault of the town. With barely five hundred men, only one hundred and seventy of whom were trained soldiers, and not a dozen even of these had ever seen real warfare, the garrison defended themselves for five long days, under the vertical sun of June; and so well did they fight, that the nawab lost five thousand men besides eighty officers.

Though surrounded on three sides by the nawab's forces, the English still retained command of the river, and when the outer defences of the settlement were driven in, most of the ladies and children were placed on board of the ships which lay off the Fort. It seems to be clear that some women and children remained in the Fort, and were among the prisoners who perished when it was taken. They were probably some of the subordinates' families, and were overlooked in the confusion, as all the officers' families were embarked safely. It had been intended that the ships should continue to lie by, and that, when the Fort could no longer be defended, the garrison should escape by the river gate and join them; but, to the endless discredit of the Governor, Mr. Drake, and the senior officers, they were seized with panic, and, hurriedly getting into the boats which lay ready, they hastened on board the ships with the announcement that all was lost. Under their orders, the ships, on the 19th of June, weighed anchor, and dropped down the river with the ebbing tide, leaving to their fate a greatly reduced garrison of brave men under John Zephaniah Holwell, the senior officer left on shore, whose courageous conduct has imperishably associated his name with the story of the Black Hole.

In spite of the desertion of the senior officers, the defence was maintained all through Sunday, the 20th of June, when only one hundred and fifty fighting men were left, and of these more than a third were wounded. Even then Holwell would have kept the enemy at bay till night, and have tried to escape down the river under cover of darkness, but, at six o'clock in the evening, a number of men, who had broken into a spirit-store and been drinking heavily, opened the river gate with the idea of escaping to the ships—the enemy at once rushed in, the stubborn resistance was broken, and Calcutta was lost.

The fighting being at an end, the nawab was carried into the Fort in his palanquin, and to him Holwell surrendered his sword, and was ordered to immediately deliver up the key of the Company's treasury. To Suraj-ud-Dowlah's great disappointment and anger, fifty thousand rupees was all the money in the treasury; he refused to believe that there was no more, and was convinced that the greater part of the vast riches which he had expected to secure must have been concealed. Twice during the evening he sent for Holwell, questioning him closely, and urging the disclosure of the concealed treasure. At the second interview he gave Holwell his assurance, on the word of a soldier, that no harm should come to the prisoners, and, ordering his officers to guard them securely for the night, he retired to rest.

The tragedy that followed is too well known in all its details to need recapitulation. It may have been caused by gross carelessness on the part of the officers in charge of the prisoners, but Holwell, whose vivid narrative of his experiences in the Black Hole is the only reliable and full account, says that it was "the result of revenge and resentment in the breasts of the lower officers, or jemadars, to whose custody the prisoners were delivered, for the number of their order killed during the siege."

Whatever may have been the reason, at about eight o'clock in the evening the prisoners were all driven into a small room which had been used as a prison for soldiers, and which was known by them as the Black Hole prison. This room was about eighteen feet square, and, situated against the curtain wall of the Fort, had no window nor door on two sides. On the third side was one small door which opened inwards, and on the fourth two small iron-barred windows. One hundred and forty-six men and women with some children, some sick, others wounded and dying, all worn out with the exertions and anxieties of the week's siege, thrust into this confined space on a sultry night in June, with the blaze of burning buildings within and around the Fort to add to the heat and dense closeness of the atmosphere were soon a prey to every horror. A fierce fever seized them, delirium set in in many cases, and the weaker members were crushed down and trodden to death in a wild struggle to reach the windows for air.

An old jemadar of the guard, seeing the desperate condition of the prisoners, and moved by Mr. Holwell's entreaties and offers of liberal reward, went twice to try and get permission to remove them to another building, but returned saying that it could not be done without an order from the nawab, who was sleeping, and no one dared to wake him. The same man, who alone showed any humanity, ordered water to be supplied to the prisoners through the windows. The unfortunate people received it eagerly in their hats thrust through the bars, but such was the struggle for a draught, that more than half was spilt and wasted before it reached their parched lips. The water only added to their sufferings, the sight of which the inhuman soldiers enjoyed, holding up blazing torches that they might see them fighting for a drink. When the maddened victims found that water but increased their agonies, they showered every imaginable abuse on their tormentors, and the nawab and his officers, in the hope of inducing the guard to fire on them and so end their sufferings, but without effect.

As the night wore on, one after another the prisoners sank and died, many even in that hour of supreme trial showing admirable calmness and fortitude. Among these were the Rev. Jervas Bellamy, the white-haired chaplain of the settlement, and his son, a young lieutenant, who laid them down hand clasped in hand and died; and Mr. Edward Eyre, a member of the Council, who, staggering over the dead, came to Mr. Holwell, and, asking him with his usual coolness and good-nature how he did, fell down and expired before he received a reply. Holwell himself, determining to die apart from the struggle at the windows, made his way back from the throng, assisted by the great strength of a ship's officer named Carey, whose girl-wife shared his prison and was the one woman who survived that night of horror. The two men laid themselves down, and poor Carey died at once; but death not coming to Holwell, his sufferings drove him to the window again. From there he once more retired, but was brought back to life and consciousness in the morning when he was drawn from under the dead and carried to the window to be shown to the nawab's officers.

Suraj-ud-Dowlah, on learning of the events of the night, sent to inquire if the chief survived, and, finding that he still breathed, he ordered the release of the unhappy remnant of his prisoners, who, scarcely able to stand, took twenty minutes to clear away the bodies of their dead comrades from against the door, so as to admit of its being opened. At six o'clock in the morning, twenty-two ghastly men and one woman staggered out from that charnel-house into the fresh morning air.

Though Suraj-ud-Dowlah may not have been primarily responsible for the inhuman massacre of his defenceless prisoners, he expressed no concern for their fate. His one thought was the treasure of which he imagined he had been cheated. Mrs. Carey and all the men, both European and native, with the exception of Messrs. Holwell, Court, Walcot and Burdet, were given their liberty; but on these four officers fell the full force of the nawab's resentment, and he ordered them to be loaded with chains and conveyed to Murshedabad, there to await his return.

The bodies of the poor creatures who perished in the Black Hole were carried out of the Fort, and thrown into the ditch of an unfinished ravelin, which the English had hastily begun opposite the main gate, but had been unable to complete before they were driven within the walls, and were covered with earth. Holwell, when he returned to Calcutta, after the town had been recovered by Clive and Admiral Watson, erected, at his own cost, over this common grave of his fellow-sufferers a monument, on which he inscribed their names and a vigorously worded record of their fate.

This monument, standing at the north-west corner of Dalhousie Square at its junction with Clive Street, was long a conspicuous object in Calcutta. Nobody, however, seemed to be responsible for its upkeep, and in the course of years it fell into disrepair and became unsightly. New sentiments and fashions had arisen too; the predominant feeling at the beginning of the nineteenth century appears to have been a desire to forget all that was disagreeable in the past, and, in 1821, the monument was taken down, and its commemorative tablet mislaid and lost.

THE HOLWELL MONUMENT AND BENGAL SECRETARIAT, 1905.

[*Face p.* 44.

The spot which should have been held sacred by every Englishman was occupied by a lamp-post, and, later, by a statue of Sir Ashley Eden. It has been reserved for the opening years of the twentieth century to see this neglect rectified, and a grave hallowed by memories of heroism and suffering once more marked by a suitable monument, a replica of the one which Holwell raised, erected by Lord Curzon in 1902, and by him presented to the city.

The same spirit of indifference which allowed the Holwell monument to perish led to the Black Hole prison being treated as an ordinary *godown*. When Calcutta was recovered by the English it was thought desirable to build an entirely new Fort, apart from the residential quarter, and the old Fort was therefore not repaired. The houses and other buildings were adapted for immediate use, and in 1766 the whole was handed over to the Customs authorities, in whose occupation it remained till 1818, when the old Fort was pulled down to make way for new warehouses. Although the Black Hole prison continued to be known by that name, and was visited by occasional sightseers, no attempt was made to preserve it as an historical spot. Lord Valentia, who visited Calcutta in 1803, wrote of it as being "part of a *godown*, or warehouse" filled with goods, so that he could not see it. When the Fort was demolished, in 1818, the site was built over and all remains obliterated.

In 1883, excavations which were made for the foundations of the East India Railway Company's Office in Fairlie Place uncovered portions of the masonry of old Fort William, and roused an interest in the identification of its exact position. Since that date additional information has been gained from time to time as old buildings have been removed and new ones erected on portions of the site, and by this means a plan of the old Fort has been constructed with reference to the position of modern buildings. These have been marked with memorial tablets to indicate the principal spots of interest, and so to keep in memory those who laid the foundations of the British Empire in India.

The oft-quoted rhyme, "Ghora pur howda Hathi pur ghin," which has so often been said to have had reference to Warren Hastings' hurried retreat from Benares to Chunar, appears to have had a much earlier origin in connection with the fall of Calcutta, and to have run—

> "Hathi pur howda, Ghora pur ghin
> Killa moorcha pur dhunka
> Calcutta lia chin."

Which may be translated—

> "Howda on elephant, saddle on horse,
> On fort bastion the war-drum
> Snatched Calcutta by force."

Very possibly a sarcastic version of the jingle may have been applied to Hastings' retreat, and it may also have been varied in the same way to suit other occasions.

Calcutta having been pillaged and the garrison destroyed or driven away, Suraj-ud-Dowlah changed the name of the town to Allynagore, and appointed a native Governor, a Hindu, Raja Manickchand. He then returned in triumph to his own capital, exacting payment as he went of large sums of money from the French and Dutch settlements at Chandernagore and Chinsurah, as the price of their exemption from similar treatment.

Holwell and his companions had, in the mean time, been carried to Murshedabad. The rains broke over Calcutta the day after its capture, and the wretched prisoners, journeying by boat, were given no shelter, but lay on a platform of bamboos at the bottom of the boat, exposed alike to the soaking rain and the scorching sun, laden with heavy fetters, covered with terrible boils the result of breathing the poisoned atmosphere during that night of agony in the Black Hole, and given only a little boiled rice for food. It is to this latter circumstance that Holwell attributed their escape from death, for, as he wrote afterwards, "could we have indulged in flesh and wine we had died beyond all doubt." Arrived at Murshedabad they were lodged in a stable near the palace, and, still laden with chains and strongly guarded, they narrowly escaped a second suffocation by "the immense crowd of spectators who came from all quarters of the city to gratify their curiosity, and blocked us up from morning till night."

On the return of the nawab to Murshedabad the old begum, his grandmother, interceded with him for the English gentlemen, and, a few days later, he ordered them to be set at liberty and allowed to go where they would; on which, as Holwell records, "as soon as our legs were free, we took boat, and proceeded to the Dutch Tanksall, where we were received and entertained with real joy and humanity."

Eventually Holwell and his companions, with Messrs. Hastings and Chambers, who had been hospitably sheltered by the French and Dutch from the time the Company's factory at Cossimbazar had been destroyed, were able to make their way down country to Fulta, where they joined the refugees from Calcutta who there awaited succour.

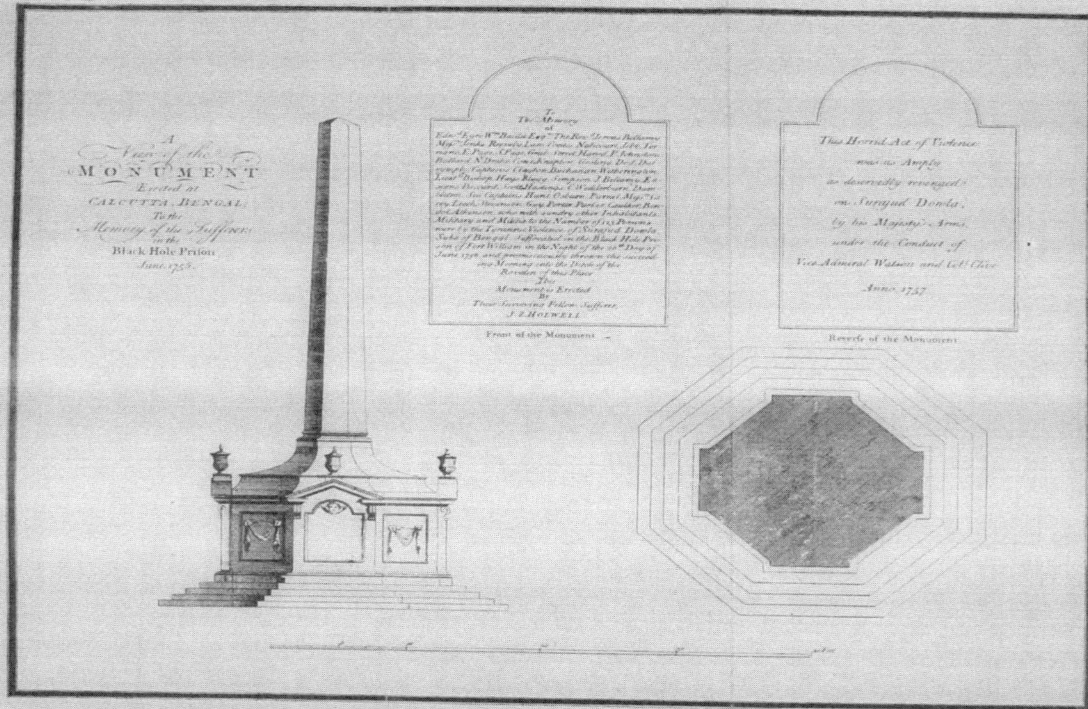

PLAN AND ELEVATION OF THE HOLWELL MONUMENT

[Face p. 42.

CHAPTER III

RECOVERY AND AFTER

The refugees at Fulta—Warren Hastings' first marriage—The recovery of Calcutta—The condition of the town and different buildings—The nawab's army—The last Battle of Calcutta—The taking of Chandernagore—"Billy" Speke—Plassey—The fate of Suraj ud-Dowlah.

WHEN Calcutta fell to the nawab's forces in June, 1756, a small fast-sailing ship hurried from the Hughly to Madras with despatches announcing the disaster. Four months later, in October, a fleet of three line-of-battle ships and eight smaller vessels sailed from Madras, bearing an avenging army of nine hundred Europeans and fifteen hundred native troops, under the joint command of Admiral Watson, and Clive—then in the early days of his fame. After numerous delays, the fleet arrived at Fulta on the 20th of December, and brought fresh hope and courage to the unfortunate people there.

Surgeon Ives, of H.M.S. *Kent*, the flag-ship of Admiral Watson, published some years later a journal of his adventures, which included the recapture of Calcutta and subsequent fighting. Of the refugees at Fulta, he wrote: "They were crowded together in the most wretched habitations, clad in the meanest apparel, surrounded by sickness and disease;" in spite of which miseries he speaks of their cheerfulness and courage as admirable. That they were by no means a prey to despair and lethargy is proved by the fact that several marriages took place in the forlorn little community. "The mutter of the dying never spoiled the lovers' kiss."

One of these marriages was that of Warren Hastings with his first wife, a lady who was long thought to have been the widow of Captain Campbell, who was killed by an accident a few days before the recovery of Calcutta. The Rev. H. B. Hyde, whose painstaking researches have thrown much light on the social history of Calcutta, found that this identification of the first Mrs. Hastings was a mistake, and that the lady was the widow of Captain John Buchanan, who, after assisting in the defence of Calcutta with much courage and ability, died in the Black Hole. His widow and baby-girl were among the refugees who escaped to Fulta, and Mr. Hyde considers it probable that Hastings married her there, and that the ceremony was performed by Admiral Watson's chaplain, Richard Cobbe, afterwards Chaplain of Calcutta in the room of the gallant old chaplain Jervas Bellamy, who perished in the Black Hole.

Mrs. Hastings died in 1759, at Cossimbazar, where her tomb still stands in the old Residency Burial-ground. Of the two children born of this marriage, a boy and a girl, the latter shared her mother's grave, the former was sent to England, where he died shortly before his father's arrival on his first visit home.

On the arrival of the Madras fleet at Fulta, the troops under Clive's command were landed on the eastern or Calcutta bank of the Hughly, and marched up to Calcutta, while Admiral Watson sailed his ships up the river.

When the troops arrived at Budge Budge they halted for the night within a short distance of a Mohammedan fort which was garrisoned by a small body of soldiers, who do not appear to have troubled themselves at all about the approach of the English. Clive proposed to attack the fort in the morning, but during the night one of the British soldiers, in a fit of drunken bravado, started off alone to reconnoitre the position. Climbing the wall of the fort unobserved, he stumbled into the midst of a party of the garrison who were beguiling their time on guard by playing cards and smoking. Taken by surprise the Mohammedans never doubted that Clive's army was upon them, and, crying to each other to save themselves, they fled precipitately, leaving the astonished soldier in possession of the fort. The story goes that the victor was reprimanded by Clive for being drunk and leaving camp, on which he exclaimed with an emphatic objurgation, that, if that was to be all the thanks he got, never again would he take a fort single-handed.

Clive's march was continued with little or no opposition, and on his reaching Calcutta, and Admiral Watson's ships sailing up at the same time to Fort William, the nawab's forces, comprising two thousand infantry and fifteen hundred cavalry, speedily retreated. On the 1st of January, 1757, the British flag was once more hoisted at Calcutta.

To punish the nawab and avenge the sack of Calcutta, the British, a few days later, advanced against Hughly, the centre of Mohammedan trade in Bengal, which town they captured and destroyed on the 10th of January. They then returned to Calcutta, and set about restoring order in the settlement, and preparing to meet Suraj-ud-Dowlah, who was collecting an immense army to march against them.

Few details can be found among the records of Calcutta as to the different buildings and their condition after the siege, but there can be no doubt that the town was in a deplorable state, owing to the wholesale and wanton destruction of property. The presence of the large body of troops added greatly to the difficulties of providing accommodation for the returned British, and for several years following the siege and recovery of Calcutta every building that could be rendered habitable was occupied to its utmost capacity.

The English church of St. Anne had been the scene of much fighting during the attack on the Fort, and was completely destroyed, but the two other churches in Calcutta, that of the Armenians, St. Nazareth, and a small Roman Catholic Church on the site of the Moorgehatta Cathedral, had both escaped uninjured. The Armenians continued to be an important section of the community, but the Roman Catholics had fallen into great disfavour. Clive, in one of his earliest reports to the court, states that the Government, immediately on their return to Calcutta, had interdicted "the public exercise of the Roman Catholic religion, and forbid the residence of their priests in our bounds." He gives as the reason for this step—

"the inconvenience we experienced at the siege of Calcutta from the prodigious number of Portuguese women who were admitted for security into the Fort, the very little or no service that race of people are of to the settlement, added to the prospect we had of a war with France, in which case we had reason to suppose they would refuse to take up arms against an enemy of their own religion should we be attacked."

The priests having been banished from the settlement, the Roman Catholic Church was available for the English chaplain, who took it over, and conducted services in it for a couple of years. By that time the interdict against the Roman Catholics had been removed by desire of the court, who disapproved of the order, and the church was restored to the priests. A temporary chapel was then fitted up for the chaplain in the gateway of the old Fort, pending the building of a new church in the new Fort, but, as events proved, it was nearly thirty years before this temporary little chapel of St. John ceased to be the presidency church.

The new Fort was naturally the first consideration, and various sites were proposed before that at Govindpore was finally selected. Captain, afterwards Sir Robert, Barker, an engineer and captain of artillery who rose to the command of the Bengal Army under Hastings in 1773-4, made a report to the board in May, 1757, on some of these suggested sites for the new Fort. As regards one of these proposals he wrote:—

"Agreeable to a request made by the Governor, I have examined the ground to the eastward of the present Fort, and am of opinion that with very little expense a proper spot of ground might be cleared about six hundred yards directly to the east of it, sufficient for a Fort, and Esplanade round it of seven or eight hundred yards. . . . Nothing more is required than an avenue to the river, which is nearly already done, and would be completely so were the houses cleared away, from the Court-house to Mr. Cooke's house, when the old Fort is pulled down."

This ground to the eastward of the old Fort, is that occupied by Lal Bazar, and the avenue to the river would have been along Dalhousie Square North. The Court-house, as we shall see later on, stood on the ground now occupied by St. Andrew's Church, St. Anne's having stood at the other end of Dalhousie Square North.

Captain Barker's report continued—

"A canal may be brought from the river close to the Fort, and have wharfs and quays, with cranes for the embarking and disembarking of goods in boats, and at the same time furnish the town with water by having pipes of communication underground to large cisterns for that purpose in the Fort; may also supply the ditches with water with proper sluices to retain or let it out at low tides. The large tank will contribute greatly to accomplishing this canal, since the length is near one-third finished to our hands."

Not the wildest dreams of the gallant captain could have imagined the busy wharves and jetties of Modern Calcutta, the mighty cranes that embark and disembark goods from monster steamers, the miles upon miles of "pipes underground" that, fed by huge cisterns, supply the requirements of the metropolis of India.

In the end this ambitious plan was put aside in favour of the simpler one of removing the village of Govindpore and building the Fort on the river bank, where the marshy plain on the land side formed a natural esplanade, and New Fort William was accordingly begun at the end of 1757. The original plans included all the public buildings within the fortifications, the

LORD CLIVE.

[*Face p.* 57.

Governor's house, Council House, officers' quarters, church, hospital, and warehouses, but, owing to difficulties in the way of labour, want of funds, and divided councils, the work proceeded but slowly, so that it was some ten years before the new Fort was completed. Long ere that period had elapsed, the position of the East India Company had entirely changed; they were no longer foreign traders, but had become the paramount power in Bengal, and a fortified factory was a thing of the past.

These changes, however, belong to later years, and Clive and Admiral Watson, when they had recaptured Calcutta, found themselves, in the opening days of 1757, confronted with many serious dangers. The nawab was marching from Murshedabad with a powerful army, Calcutta was in no condition to resist the attack, and, to add to the difficulties of the situation, France and England were on the eve of war, and the French at Chandernagore might at any moment move against the English settlement.

The English forces comprised some seven hundred European infantry; fifteen hundred sepoys, lately raised for the first time; eight hundred artillery with fourteen guns, nearly all 6-pounders; and the sailors from the fleet.

Suraj-ud-Dowlah's army mustered eighteen thousand horse, fifteen thousand foot, ten thousand *Bildars* or Pioneers, forty pieces of heavy artillery drawn by oxen, fifty elephants, and an armed rabble of followers. This huge army crossed the river near Hughly, and, approaching Calcutta from the Dum Dum side, settled like a swarm of locusts on the villages which skirted the settlement.

A little to the south of where the Dum Dum Road then, as now, entered the town, stood the houses of two wealthy natives, Govindram Mittre, and Omichand. At the time the Mahratta Ditch was dug, it was carried round these two houses, although they lay outside its course, so as to include them in its protection. The nawab on reaching Calcutta established his head-quarters in Omichand's garden, leaving his body-guard of Mogul horse on the opposite side of the Ditch, with the main body of the army, whose outskirts extended nearly as far south as Ballygunge. On learning of the isolated position of the nawab's personal camp, Clive formed the bold plan to make a night attack on the enemy's artillery, spike the guns, and then, in the confusion, attack Suraj-ud-Dowlah's head-quarters, and thus strike terror into his army. The plan, though considerably altered in its execution, was entirely successful in its effect, and on the 5th of February, 1757, was fought the last battle of Calcutta, which left the British undisputed masters of their settlement.

When the nawab's army was marching on Calcutta, Clive formed an entrenched camp near Cossipore, about half a mile inland from the river. Here he placed a small force of Europeans and three hundred sepoys, an equal number garrisoned the Fort, the remainder were available for active operations. At three o'clock on the morning of Saturday, the 5th of February, Clive marched his column from the Cossipore camp, in a dense fog such as is common in Calcutta during the cold season. Four hundred sepoys led the way, an equal number brought up the rear, in the middle were six hundred and fifty European infantry and one hundred artillery. A body of six hundred sailors drew the guns, guarded them, and took charge of the lascars who carried the ammunition, and who would otherwise have deserted.

Marching silently through the fog, the leading troops surprised the enemy's outposts, who, after a hurried discharge of matchlocks and rockets, fled in confusion. Unfortunately one of the rockets struck a sepoy, and exploded his pouch of cartridges, setting fire to some of his comrades and disorganizing the advance for a time. When the march was resumed the leaders had lost their bearings, and the enemy's battery was missed: the column, however, marched steadily on through the fog, till they arrived opposite Suraj-ud-Dowlah's headquarters in Omichand's garden, but on the opposite side of the Ditch. Now for the first time an attempt was made to check their advance, and the Mogul horse bore down on them, but as they charged through the fog a deadly fire swept their ranks, they checked, swerved, and fled in disorder.

Clive's plan was to seize a causeway which crossed the Ditch into the town, a little to the south of Omichand's garden, on the line of the present road which passes the Gas Works, and, turning back from there, to fall on the nawab's camp. With this intention the march was continued rapidly, the guns in the middle of the column firing obliquely forward into the fog on either side, and the troops keeping up a discharge of musketry against the unseen foe. Thus dealing dismay and death around, the British reached the causeway without a check. But then occurred a fatal blunder. As the leading troops turned upon the causeway they came into the line of the fire of their own guns, and, before the firing could be stopped, several men had been killed and the whole column thrown into confusion. By this time the fog was beginning to lighten, and, before the troops could be re-formed and led to the attack of a barricade at the end of the causeway, they were suddenly swept by a deadly fire from two heavy guns, which, mounted in a small bastion in the lines along the Ditch, had been unsuspected in the darkness.

It was impossible to assault the barricade in the face of this fire, and the column hastily resumed the march beside the Ditch, making for the next causeway—that which carried the road which, leading to the main gate of the old Fort, was known successively as the Avenue and the Great Bungalow Road before it took its present name of Bow Bazar Street. The position was now one of great peril: the country to be crossed was a succession of rice-fields, dry and cracked at that season of the year, and divided by innumerable little banks over which the guns had to be dragged. The enemy's guns continued to fire on the column, which as it advanced came into range of two other guns, mounted in a similar position at the other causeway, while the Mogul cavalry, emboldened by seeing the weakness of the little force, made several charges on the rear.

With stubborn courage the British pressed on, keeping the enemy at bay, pausing from time to time to return the fire of the guns, till at last they reached the road and formed their ranks to attack the nawab's troops, both cavalry and infantry, who held the passage of the Ditch. In this they were splendidly successful—the infantry at once gave way before the assault, the cavalry did little better, though, closing on the rear, they captured a gun, only to surrender it again to a charge led by Ensign Yorke. Having cleared the passage, the column quickly crossed over, and marching along the Avenue—Bow Bazar—they shook off the pursuing troops, and reached the Fort before midday. From there they marched again in the evening, and returned by the river-bank to the camp at Cossipore. The scene of the last engagement with the nawab's troops lies within the boundaries of the terminus of the Eastern Bengal Railway at Sealdah.

The English losses in the operations numbered twenty-seven Europeans, eighteen sepoys, and twelve sailors killed; and seventy Europeans, thirty-five sepoys, and twelve sailors wounded. Among the killed were Clive's A.D.C., Captain Bridges, and his secretary, Mr. Belcher. The nawab's casualties numbered thirteen hundred killed and wounded, besides four elephants, five hundred horses, and three hundred draught cattle. The result was all that Clive could have hoped; the nawab retired in panic from the neighbourhood of Calcutta, and, camping near Dum Dum, sent conciliatory messages to Clive, offering to make restitution for the destruction of Calcutta, and professing a desire to conclude a friendly alliance with the British—offers to which the Calcutta Government were glad to make a favourable response.

The nawab's retreat having relieved the British commanders of their immediate anxiety, they turned their thoughts to securing themselves against French hostilities. They first proposed to the Governor of Chandernagore that the French and English settlements in Bengal should remain neutral; but to this the Governor felt himself unable to agree, as he was under the orders of the Governor of Pondicherry. Admiral Watson and Clive thereupon decided to take the initiative, and, obtaining a reluctant permission from Suraj-ud-Dowlah to attack Chandernagore, the British ships sailed up the Hughly, and, after some severe fighting, captured the French settlement on the 23rd of March. On the following day the English wounded were brought down to Calcutta, and most of them placed in the hospital under the care of Surgeon Ives, of H.M.S. *Kent*.

The hospital appears to have escaped destruction during the siege and occupation of Calcutta. It stood apart from the Fort, on the ground now occupied by Garstin's Place, in close contiguity to the burying-ground, which must have been a fruitful source of disease and death to the unfortunate patients.

Among those wounded at Chandernagore were Captain Henry Speke, of the *Kent*, and his son William, a lad of sixteen, who was serving as midshipman on his father's ship. Ives, who was on the *Kent* tending the wounded during the action, gives in his *Journal* a long and pathetic account of poor Billy Speke's sufferings and death, and of the distress of his wounded father. It was the same shot which struck down both father and son: the captain was not dangerously wounded, but the poor boy had a leg almost torn off, the shattered limb hanging only by the skin when he was carried down to the surgeon in the arms of a quarter-master, who, while carrying the wounded lad, was himself killed by a cannon ball. The devoted son would not allow his wounds to be dressed till his father had been attended to, and bore the amputation

ADMIRAL CHARLES WATSON.

[*Face p.* 65.

of his leg and subsequent sufferings with equal patience and heroism. Captain Speke recovered from his wound, but poor little Billy died in the hospital a fortnight later, of tetanus. He was buried in the adjoining burial-ground, now St. John's Churchyard, where his tomb remains in good preservation, with its curiously worded epitaph as follows—

HERE LYES THE
BODY OF WILLIAM SPEKE
AGED 18 SON OF HY. SPEKE ESQR.
CAPTAIN OF HIS MAJESTY'S SHIP KENT
HE LOST HIS LEG AND LIFE IN THAT SHIP
AT THE CAPTURE OF FORT ORLEANS
THE 24TH MARCH ANNO 1757.

This inscription gives the boy's age as eighteen, whereas Ives says he was sixteen, and the date of the capture of Chandernagore is also wrongly stated, as the town was taken on the 23rd of March. Near Billy Speke's tomb is that of Admiral Watson, who died on the 16th of August, 1757, at the early age of forty-four.

Before Admiral Watson died, Clive had led his conquering army to Plassey and Murshedabad. The reasons which led to this change of policy are matters of history. Suraj-ud-Dowlah, while keeping at a respectful distance from Calcutta, had broken faith with the English, and was intriguing with the French to come up from

Southern India, and oust the English from Bengal. The leading nobles at Murshedabad were disgusted with the folly and tyranny of their young ruler, and the commander in-chief of his army, Meer Jaffir, opened negotiations with Clive to overthrow the nawab, and elect him in his room. The office of nawab had never been an hereditary one, and from time immemorial might had been right in the country, so that the proposal was quite in keeping with the traditions of native government, and Clive willingly entered into a treaty which promised safety and prosperity to the country under a stable government.

In the middle of June, 1757, Clive marched against Murshedabad. The nawab, alternating between defiance and terror, advanced with his army to meet the British, and, on the 23rd June, near the little village of Plassey, the two armies met, and the victory which made secure the foundations of the British Empire in India was won. The defeated Suraj-ud-Dowlah mounted a swift camel, and, accompanied by some two thousand of his army, fled to Murshedabad, leaving in his camp at Plassey several hundred women, who, according to Verelst, "Meer Jaffir sent to offer to Col. Clive."

From his deserted palace the stricken nawab fled again at midnight with the very few faithful women and servants who still followed his fortunes, and attempted to make his way up the river in boats, hoping to find an asylum in the northern provinces. But past misdeeds now rose against him : the party stopped to try and procure food at the cell of a Mohammedan recluse; this man, remembering a wanton insult received from the nawab in the past, detained the fugitives with promises of assistance, while he sent information of their presence to the new nawab, Jaffir Khan. The unhappy Suraj-ud-Dowlah, so long the petted and spoilt child of Fortune, was seized and carried back to Murshedabad, where, within a few days of the first anniversary of the Massacre of the Black Hole, he was murdered in cold blood as he lay fettered in a dungeon.

With the death of Suraj-ud-Dowlah the troubles of the English were at an end. The new nawab lost no time in sending to Calcutta the indemnity promised to the inhabitants for their losses and sufferings. From the depths of poverty and humiliation they were raised at once to wealth and power. The town gave itself up to general rejoicing, and at this happy time, says Orme, "Quarrels were forgotten and enemies became friends."

CHAPTER IV

PUBLIC BUILDINGS

Calcutta buildings in the eighteenth century—Government House—The Council House—Court House—Hospital—Burying-ground—Old Church and the Rev. Kiernander—The New Fort and Hastings.

WITH the triumphant reversal of fortune which followed Plassey, the necessity for keeping the English factory at Calcutta within the Fort was at an end. The town at once began to expand, and the European quarter to spread. At first, as was natural, new houses were built along the roads which already existed, chief among them "the Avenue"—Bow Bazar,—and the pilgrim road, Chowringhee, from which they diverged into Dhurrumtolla and Jaun Bazar. The wide spaces between these main lines were covered with villages, fields, tanks and watercourses, which year by year gave way before the advancing town, till at last the only traces of the old order that remained were to be found in the names of different divisions of the town, and in the *bustees* which in ever-dwindling numbers still lingered among the streets. Bow Bazar with its spacious width was long a fashionable quarter, and many of the old houses, given up now to squalor and decay, still show traces of their ancient splendour in their large and lofty rooms, beneath whose decorated ceilings ladies in hooped skirts and powdered hair once tripped lightly in the dance with gallant partners brave in lace ruffles and wigs, or passed through the tall doors and down the wide stairs to their sedan chairs or high swinging chariots, to be marshalled home by *mussalchies* with flaming torches.

The house which Clive occupied on the recovery of Calcutta, and from which Clive Street took its name, is thought by Doctor Busteed to have stood about the site of the present Royal Exchange, and to have been the house "behind the Play House" which Philip Francis rented, in 1776, at £100 per month. The following extract from a private diary, under date of October, 1795, would suggest rather that Clive's house stood in Lyons Range. The entry, which is in reference to a survey of the house in question on behalf of an intending purchaser, is as follows:—

"28th October, 1795. To Williamson's; it is Hamilton's house behind the Writers' Buildings. After examining the house carefully, I advised him to have nothing to do with it, either to repair it or purchase it. He wants a regular survey to be held upon it, so recommended him to call in Tiretta (Civil Architect).

"October 30th, 1795. Tiretta called; accompanied him to G. Williamson's. Tiretta is for building two rooms, I am for pulling the whole down; for to obtain these two upper rooms, he must build four, namely the two lower ones also, and these certainly at a loss, for they can never be put to any use, being so low, only level with the compound. Williamson said it was the Government House when he came out, but believes it was taken for that purpose merely because it had doors and windows to it; the Mohammedans had burnt those of other houses at the capture of Calcutta."

From the above description it seems clear that this cannot have been the house which Francis called "the best house in the town" when he rented it twenty years earlier, and Dr. Busteed's identification of the site of the Royal Exchange as the position of this latter house is probably correct. In the "Plan of the Territory of Calcutta in 1742," given as an inset in Upjohn's map, "Mr. Eyre's house" is shown to the north of St. Anne's Church, the position described by the diarist as "behind Writers' Buildings." In Upjohn's own map, 1792–3, what was presumably the same house is shown with the new Theatre adjoining it on the west, "Theatre Street" running between the two. The Theatre stood on the site of the present new China Bazar, which makes the position of the house correspond with the corner of the road from the Bazar into Lyons Range, and it is safe to conjecture that this was the house described in 1776, in the deeds relating to the lease of the land on which Writers' Buildings was built, as "the house in the occupation of James Huggins, merchant." Clive most likely occupied "Mr. Eyre's house," if such it was, during the three years of his first administration of Bengal, from January, 1757, to February, 1760, when he sailed for England, and lived in the larger and probably new house during his second administration.

The Governor's residence within the Fort was in ruins after the siege, and his private house outside the walls was too much injured for immediate occupation. It had been used as an outpost, but was abandoned on the second day of the siege. The house is said by Long to have been reoccupied as Government House, and to have been in so decayed and ruinous a condition in 1767, when it was surveyed by the Civil Architect, as to require immediate and thorough repair. It appears doubtful, to say the least, if the house referred to in the architect's report as "Government House" was the Governor's house of Drake's time, 1756, as in a letter to the court, dated December 31, 1758, the Calcutta Council report that they had "purchased Mr. Drake's house for the sum of twelve thousand rupees, to be used as an import warehouse when the old Fort was clearing out to be converted into barracks for the military." (These barracks were for use till the new Fort was completed.) It seems more likely that the Governor's house thus purchased was identical with the Bankshall of later years, which was pulled down in 1812, when it was in a state past repair. The present Small Cause Court occupies the site of the old Bankshall: an examination of old maps shows that the old building stood on the river's bank; this was conclusively proved in 1890, when the western extension of the Court was being built. The excavations then made for foundations revealed masonry remains, which were easily identified as a portion of the southern wall of the "New Dock" which was built adjoining the Bankshall just one hundred years earlier, in 1790, and was filled up in 1808.

It is not clear where "Government House" stood up to 1789, when M. Grandpré, a French officer who published an account of his "Voyage

GOVERNMENT HOUSE AND COUNCIL HOUSE, CALCUTTA, 1794.

[Face p. 73.

in the Indian Ocean and to Bengal," wrote of the Governor at Calcutta as living in a house on the Esplanade, "handsome, but by no means equal to what it ought to be for a personage of so much importance." This house on the Esplanade was figured in a coloured engraving, one of a set published by Baillie in 1794, which shows it to have stood at the junction of Government Place East and the Esplanade. The house faced the Esplanade, which at that time ran continuously from Dhurrumtolla Street to the river, and it could only have been by a stretch of courtesy that the gallant visitor described it as "handsome."

As shown in the engraving, it was an ordinary house of two storeys, with a closed verandah on the upper floor and an arched one below. On the balustraded terrace was a single room with a sloping roof, apparently a wooden structure. At either end of the house was a wing in which were probably the A.D.C.'s and other officers' quarters. These wings formed a courtyard in front of the house, from which two square pillared gateways opened on to the Esplanade, and between them ran a low masonry wall surmounted by a light wooden railing. The house was so small that all public entertainments given by the Governor were held at the Court House, which was long the centre of Calcutta social gatherings; and so pinched was the accommodation for the household, that Lord Cornwallis, in 1793, rented a house in Old Court House Street, at Rs. 500 a month, for the use of his staff.

Adjoining Government House, to the west, stood the Council House, the two buildings together occupying the width of the present Government House grounds. For a twelvemonth after the recovery of Calcutta there was no Council Room, as is shown by the "Consultations" for June 22, 1758, when it was agreed that—

"there being at present no proper places for the public offices, from which circumstance many inconveniences arise in carrying out the business of the settlement, and as it will be proper likewise to have a room to hold our Councils in contiguous to the Secretary's and Accountant's Offices, the dwelling-house of the late Mr. Richard Court be purchased for the Honble. Company, and appropriated to the above uses."

It is not likely that this house of Mr. Court's could have been to the south of "the Creek," as at that date, 1758, the settlement was only just beginning to extend on that side. It was probably a house near the hospital, and remained in use till 1764, when the Council House on the

Esplanade was built, and gave its name to the street which led to it from the other public offices round the "Great Tank." The Proceedings for October 15, 1764, record that—

> "the present Council Room being from its situation greatly exposed to the heat of the weather, and from its vicinity to the Public Offices very ill calculated for conducting the business of the Board with that privacy which is often requisite, it is agreed to build a new Council Room at a convenient distance from the offices."

Having experienced the heat of the weather in their old quarters, the Board selected an open situation which enjoyed the full benefit of the southerly breeze across the Esplanade of the New Fort, which by that time was nearing completion, and "contiguous" to it they built, either then or later, a house for the Governor. These two buildings continued in use till 1799, when the magnificent Marquis Wellesley built the present Government House, on the site which they had occupied.

Another public institution for which new quarters had to be found was the hospital. The old building adjoining the burial-ground was a veritable death-trap to those unfortunates who were driven to seek its shelter, and had been the subject of constant complaint for years. At last, in 1768, a house was purchased from a native gentleman for the purpose of a hospital. It stood to the south of the Esplanade, the Maidan, practically in the country. This house, with various alterations and additions including two other buildings erected in 1795, remained in use as the Presidency General Hospital up to the last few years, when it made way for a new hospital on the same site, in keeping with the requirements of modern science.

The considerations of public health which suggested the removal of the hospital to a more open situation and purer air led also to the closing of the old burial-ground, and the opening of the new cemetery at a distance from the town, that now known as South Park Street Cemetery. The records of the "Consultations" for the 25th of August, 1767, contain this entry: "The President acquainted the Board that, the New Burying Ground near Mr. Vansittart's garden being now ready, they desired the clergyman to consecrate it, as the sickly season is approaching"—a reference to the fever which prevailed at the close of the rains.

On the same date—August 25, 1767—the first interment took place in this ground, that of

Mr. John Wood, a writer in the Council House. The monument over this grave was levelled some years later, when an addition was made to the ground, and the oldest tomb that remained was that of Mrs. Sarah Pearson, aged 19, who died on the 8th of September, 1767. It would appear, however, that the ground at this time had not been consecrated, for, on the 18th of May following, the chaplain, the Rev. William Parry, submitted a letter to the President and Council representing that the great distance of the New Burial Ground from Calcutta, "which I am required to consecrate for immediate use (if required), obliges me to request that you would please to make such an allowance for bearers to attend duty there as you may judge necessary and sufficient for that purpose." The allowance the Board judged sufficient for the reverend gentleman's palkee-bearers was thirty rupees a month, which amount was accordingly added to the chaplain's salary.

Palkee-bearers were at this time regular members of every household staff of servants, and a simple little joke of a clerical brother of Chaplain Parry, the Rev. J. Z. Kiernander, who spoke of his palankeen and bearers as his "coach and four," served to point a moral for many who took the worthy pastor in a literal sense, as even

Dr. Busteed has done in later years, and shook their heads over his unbecoming extravagance, when the poor man fell into pecuniary difficulties, as he did in the closing years of his long missionary career. To the Rev. John Zachary Kiernander belongs the credit of having built what is now the oldest Protestant church in Calcutta—the Old or Mission Church—the second oldest place of Christian worship, the Armenian church being the oldest. Kiernander himself was the first Protestant missionary in Bengal; he came to Calcutta in 1758, from Tranquebar, at the instance of the S.P.C.K., in whose missions in Madras he had been working for eighteen years, and with the cordial approval, if not the direct invitation, of Clive. Kiernander was warmly welcomed in Calcutta, and received the friendly support of the Company's chaplain, the Rev. Henry Butler, who assisted him in obtaining subscriptions for the mission work.

It is not very creditable to the Calcutta community of that period and the Court of Directors that, after the destruction of St. Anne's Church in 1756, no English church was erected in the town till Kiernander built his Mission Church in 1770, and there was no Presidency church till 1787, when St. John's Church was completed. When Kiernander arrived in Calcutta Mr. Butler was holding the English services in the Portuguese Chapel, the Roman Catholic priests having been temporarily banished from the settlement. This chapel was a small and damp brick building on the site now occupied by the Moorgehatta Cathedral, and here Kiernander, with the chaplain's permission, instituted a Sunday service in Portuguese, his Mission being addressed primarily to the Portuguese Roman Catholics, of whom there were an immense number in Calcutta.

These people, who formed the poorest class of natives, were descendants for the most part of the Portuguese adventurers and soldiers who had come to Bengal in the sixteenth and seventeenth centuries. It was always the policy of the Portuguese commanders in India to encourage marriages between their soldiers and the women of the country, with the idea of strengthening their rule by ties of interest and affection. At the same time, they steadily refused all official employment to the children of such marriages, and even debarred the children of Portuguese parents who were born in India from the higher offices of Government. Such a policy naturally worked its own ruin; the bolder and more enterprising members of the mixed community, disowned by their father's race, outcasts from their mother's kindred, repaid contempt with hate, and, taking to piracy and brigandage, became a terror to those who had outlawed them. While the more timid, priding themselves on their European descent, and clinging to a pitiful imitation of European customs, were driven to menial occupations for a livelihood, and, sinking deeper and deeper in the social scale, made the proud Portuguese names they had inherited a byword through the land for all that was vicious, idle, and degraded. Kiernander's mission work early bore fruit; during his first year in Calcutta he had the satisfaction of receiving fifteen converts, while during the twenty-eight years of his mission in Bengal he baptized over five hundred adult converts, Hindu as well as Portuguese.

Kiernander's wife, a sister of Colonel Fischer of the Madras Army, accompanied him to Calcutta, where she died three years later. A year after her death he married a wealthy widow, a Mrs. Ann Woolley, and at about the same time he received a legacy on the death of a brother in Sweden. This with his first wife's fortune placed him in comfortable circumstances, and in 1767, when his congregation had largely increased, he decided to erect a church at his own expense. The "Mission Church" was accordingly built, at a cost of over sixty-seven thousand rupees, of which sum Kiernander provided all but about two thousand rupees which was subscribed by sympathizers. The architect was a Dane, Martin Boutant de Mevell, and the church he raised was a bare and barnlike structure, very unlike what it is now, after undergoing various alterations and enlargements since its completion in 1770.

The church was consecrated under the name Beth Tephilla (House of Prayer), but the clumsy appellation seems never to have been used, and after other churches were built it was called simply the Old Church, a name by which it has been known by successive generations to the present day. The red-brick exterior of the church is said to have gained for it the name of Lal Girja, or Red Church, from the natives. It is sometimes said that the Dalhousie Square tank took its native name Lal Diggee, the Red Tank, from a red-brick bastion of the Old Fort which, reflected in its waters, gave them a ruddy appearance. Whether this was so, or the tank was known to the natives, as it certainly was to the early English, as the Great Tank is an open question. The name Lal Diggee may have been acquired later from the Lal Girja, in the same way as that of the upper part of Bow Bazar, Lal Bazar, was. It must be remembered that when Kiernander built his church there were no houses between it and the tank. One of the set of Baillie's engravings of 1794, already alluded to, gives a view of "Tank Square" which shows the church clearly. It is interesting to note, in view of the large buildings recently erected at this end of Old Court House Street, that, up to May, 1806, a restraint lay on this ground from building upper-roomed houses—a restriction possibly imposed long before, in connection with the Old Fort.

In addition to building the church, Kiernander erected a school-house and minister's house adjoining the church; and when, in 1773, his second wife died, he buried her in a plot of land adjoining the burial-ground in Park Street, which he purchased and devoted to the use of the Mission congregation. Kiernander had evidently a weakness for bricks and mortar, for in addition to the Mission buildings he built for himself a house in Camac Street, which he called Beth Saron, and a "garden house" at Bhowanipore, which he named Saron Grove, and which now forms a portion of the premises of the London Missionary Society. Unfortunately for himself, Kiernander's eldest son shared his father's taste, and, in 1787, he induced the old man to stand security for a large sum of money which he raised for the purpose of building houses, a form of speculation greatly in vogue at the time. Before the buildings were completed young Kiernander's creditors pressed for payment, and, finding him unable to meet their demand, they took alarm, and had his property attached and sold at a ruinous loss. The property of the elder Kiernander, as his son's security, was also seized, and the sheriff's seal was placed upon the Mission Church, the school-house, and the burial-ground. At this deplorable juncture a member of the Mission Church congregation, Mr. Charles Grant, of the Company's Civil Service, came forward to rescue the Mission buildings. The church, school-house, and burial-ground, which had cost altogether a lakh of rupees, were assessed at one-tenth of that sum only. Mr. Grant paid ten thousand rupees for the property, which he placed in the hands of three trustees on behalf of the Mission, and thus saved from partition, and perhaps destruction, the outcome of years of devoted toil.

The Kiernanders left Calcutta for the Dutch settlement of Chinsurah, where the old missionary was appointed chaplain, and where he remained till 1795, when the town passed into the hands of the English. His son had died in the interval, leaving a widow and young family, with whom the old man returned to Calcutta, where the last few years of his life passed peacefully. He died in 1799, at the great age of eighty-eight, aud was laid to rest in the family vault he had prepared in the Mission Burial Ground, in Park Street. While Kiernander was the first Protestant missionary to Bengal, his successor, the Rev. A. T. Clarke, was the first Protestant missionary of English nationality in Bengal, his arrival, in 1789, preceding by four years that of the Baptist missionary, Dr. Carey, for whom the honour is sometimes claimed.

One of the earliest duties Mr. Kiernander took up on his arrival in Calcutta was the charge of the Charity School, which he continued to conduct without payment for nearly twenty years, when advancing age and failing sight obliged him to resign. This Charity School, which in 1800 was amalgamated with the Calcutta Free School, was founded, as far back as 1727, by public subscription for the purpose of "educating poor European children in the Protestant religion." Mr. Richard Bourchier, a member of the Calcutta Council and Master Attendant, afterwards Governor of Bombay, took a leading part in founding the school; and when, shortly after, a Mayor's Court was established in Calcutta, this gentleman built a Court House for its accommodation, which he made over to the Government on

THE OLD COURT HOUSE, ABOUT 1784.

[*Face p.* 85.

condition that they paid £400 a year as rent to the funds of the Charity School. The Court House which Mr. Bourchier built stood for sixty years on the site where St. Andrew's Church now stands; it appears not to have been seriously injured during the siege of the town, and, as the Mayor's Court only occupied a part of the building, the remainder was available for various purposes. In 1762 the Court House was greatly enlarged by the addition of verandahs twenty-five feet broad to both floors on the south, an additional saloon with a room at each end, arches opening all around, and a dancing-saloon, "in order that it might be used as an exchange, post-office, quarter-sessions office, public entertainments and assembly-rooms," and the rent, which at this time was two thousand rupees a year, proportionately increased. It continued to increase from time to time, till, in 1778, it rose to eight hundred sicca rupees a month. These were the best days of the old house: the Mayor's Court had been abolished a few years before, and gradually the tide of fashion ebbed away to rival assembly-rooms, the theatre, and other places of entertainment; the floors became unsafe for dancing, and, finally, the "Old Court House" was pulled down in 1792, and only its name remains commemorated in Old Court House

Street. For more than twenty years the site remained vacant, till, in 1815, it was given by the Government for the Scotch Church.

During the years in which these changes were taking place and transforming Calcutta from a trading factory to a city, Fort William was gradually approaching completion. There had been considerable trouble with contractors and skilled labourers, and a large number of bricklayers and artificers were sent out from England by the Court of Directors "for the better carrying on of the works." These men received wages ranging from £60 to £90 a year, but, owing to the large number of houses which were being built and the consequent demand for labour, they were able to command much higher salaries from private employers, so that, in 1766,—

"the Committee of Works complained that out of nine hundred or one thousand bricklayers formerly in the Company's pay, all but twenty-three had been seduced into private employ by higher pay, and they asked for an order that the price of all labour should be determined by what the Company pay, and all skilled labourers should be registered and private persons be allowed to employ them only as they can be spared."

It would be interesting to know if the native

term "mistery," applied to skilled workmen and artisans, took its origin at this time from the imported English workmen. The following suggestive passage occurs in Lofties' "London:"—

"No other city has permitted such a development of its misteries and trades, nowhere else in England have chartered associations of the kind attained such wealth and power. The very word 'mistery' often mis-spelled 'mystery,' implies skilled knowledge, or mastery of a branch of industrial art."

The very large number of English workmen, of every grade, employed for so many years on the building of the Fort, could not but make an impression on the great army of inferior workmen and coolies associated with them, and must have wrought a great change in Bengalee methods, while adopting all that was best and most suited to the climate.

It was at this period that the isolated little suburb of Hastings was formed, in the first instance as a temporary settlement for the workmen, and later as convenient for the dwellings of subordinates connected with the Fort. It was long known by its original native name of *Coolie Bazar*, but received its present style in later years from its proximity to Hastings Bridge over Tolly's Nullah, built in 1833, and named in honour of the Marquis of Hastings, under whose auspices the first iron bridge in India, a foot-bridge, had been erected in 1822, over Tolly's Nullah at Kalighat.

This iron bridge had a span of 141 feet, but was only 8 feet wide, and was approached by a steep causeway, being intended only for foot-passengers and pack bullocks. A carriage bridge was built in 1891, a little to the north of the old bridge, which was then pulled down, when a copper plate bearing the following inscription was removed from the structure :—

"Under the auspices of the most noble Francis, Marquess of Hastings, etc., etc., Governor-General and Commander-in-Chief in India, this Iron Bridge, the first of the description in India, is erected.

Lt. G. Aug. Schalch, Act. Mas. Mas.,
Anno Domini 1822,
June 1st;
Anno Lucio 5226."

CHAPTER V

IN HASTINGS' DAY

Jaffir Ali's deposition, and residence at Alipore—Hastings' connection with Alipore ; his second wife—Mrs. Hastings' town house —Mrs. Fay and her house—Francis and his houses—The site of the duel—Major Tolly and "Belvedere," and Tolly's Nullah.

IN 1760, three years after the battle of Plassey, the Nawab Jaffir Ali Khan, who had been created nawab by Clive, was deposed by Clive's successor in the Government, Mr. Vansittart, and his son-in-law, Meer Cossim, was made nawab in his room. The deposed nawab petitioned the Calcutta Board for permission, which was readily granted, to reside in Calcutta, on the ground that he "could not be safe in Bengal excepting under English protection." He accordingly took up his residence in the neighbourhood which has since been known as Alipore. It was a custom of Mohammedan rulers to rename any town or locality which they might occupy, and the distinctly Mohammedan name of Alipore, among the Hindu villages of Bhowanipore, Durgapore, and Kalighat, tells of an alien occupation, while any doubt that might remain is dispelled by the names which still cling to plots of land in the neighbourhood, such as *Begumbari* and *Sahiba-began.*

The exact site in Alipore where Jaffir Ali lived during the three years of his exile may be open to question, but it is permissible to conjecture that his house stood near where now stands the Court of the Judge of the Twenty-four Pergunnahs, and that, when his period of deposition came to an end in 1763, the house, and grounds, and adjoining lands passed into the hands of Warren Hastings. It seems probable that the nawab presented the property to Hastings as a gift, as a return possibly for kindness and attention received. That his was a grateful nature is shown by the terms of his legacy to Clive, to whom he owed his elevation to the *gadi*, which ran as follows:—

"Three lacs fifty thousand rupees in money, fifty thousand rupees in jewels, and one lac in Gold Mohurs, in all Five lacs of rupees in money and effects to the Light of my eyes, the Nabob firm in war, Lord Clive the Hero."

This magnificent legacy Clive, as is well

WARREN HASTINGS.

[*Face p.* 91.

known, devoted to the establishing of a fund for the support of disabled officers and soldiers, and the widows of officers and soldiers.

Whether by gift or by purchase, the house and land in question were acquired by Warren Hastings, and in 1763, the year in which Jaffir Ali left Alipore on his re-instatement as nawab, Hastings requested "permission of the Board to build a bridge over the Kalighat (Tolly's) Nullah, on the road to his garden house"—which request was complied with.

"Hastings House," Alipore, was the house which Hastings built in later years, and which he occupied up to the time he left India finally. The house which he first acquired lay to the west of "Hastings House," and the grounds included the whole of the land lying within the sweep of the public road. The number of houses built in this neighbourhood during recent years, and the opening of the Judges Court Road, which divides the original block, have so altered this locality that it is difficult now to trace the boundaries which a few years back it was comparatively easy to define. Some years ago Dr. Busteed, in an interesting article contributed to the *Calcutta Englishman* of the 27th of May, 1892, transcribed an advertisement which he had found in a file of the *Calcutta*

Gazette for 1785, in the British Museum. The advertisement ran as follows :—

"To be sold by Messrs. Williams and Lee, at the Old Court House on the 10th May next (a map of estate now lying for inspection at the Library), part of the estate of W. Hastings at Alipur, in 3 lots :

"Lot 1. The house opposite the paddock gate consisting of hall, a large verandah to the southward, and six rooms. Two small bungalows, large tank of excellent water, and above 63 biggas of land, partly lawn, but chiefly garden ground in high cultivation, and well stocked with a great variety of fruit trees.

"Lot. 2. An upper-roomed house consisting of hall and 2 rooms on each floor, a handsome stone staircase and a back staircase all highly finished with Madras chunam and the very best materials. A lower-roomed house containing a large hall and four good bed chambers: a complete bathing-house containing 2 rooms finished with Madras chunam: a convenient bungalow containing 2 rooms and a verandah all round, a large range of pucka buildings containing stabling for 14 horses, and 4 coach houses: other stables also (thatched) for 12 horses and 6 carriages, and 46 biggas of ground.

"Lot 3. The paddock, containing 52 biggas of ground surrounded with railed fence."

It is this advertisement to which Hastings alluded in one of his letters to his wife, who had preceded him to England, when he said, "I have actually advertised the sale of it in three lots, the old house and garden forming one, the new house and outhouses the second, and the paddock the third. I have parted with all my mares, except four which have colts."

The three parcels of land described in the advertisement formed one unbroken block, and the three lots were identified in the columns of the *Englishman* as follows :—

"When Warren Hastings' landed property at Alipore was sold in 1785 in three lots, the purchasers of the first two lots were Messrs. Turner and Jackson respectively : the third lot, the paddock, was purchased by a Mr. Honeycomb, an attorney of the Supreme Court. Some fifty years later 'the paddock' was acquired by D. W. H. Speede, the founder of the well-known arrow-root works, and he changed the name from the paddock to 'the Penn,' an obvious synonym, and so confused what was an unmistakable record of the old time. At the time of the transfer of the paddock to Honeycomb, the title-deeds were accompanied by a letter referring to the original grant of the land to Hastings. This letter was forwarded some years ago to the India Office by the present occupier of the property, through whose courtesy many of the above facts have been obtained."

Still further changes have taken place during the last decade, and with the disappearance of the old "Penn" has gone the last trace of the past, for the modern residences which have arisen on the site have nothing in common with the old paddock in which Hastings' mares and their foals ran free.

The first lot, described in the advertisement, was the land lying to the west of Hastings House, and extending as far as Alipore Road. This ground, which is now divided by Judges' Court Road, and on which the Judges' Court House and other houses now stand, was at that time one unbroken block of sixty-three *biggas.* It was laid out in lawns and gardens, in which were planted cinnamon and other rare and valuable trees, which Hastings was desirous of introducing into Bengal. Separating this lot from "the Penn," or paddock, was a drive, leading to the principal gate of Hastings House; this is now a branch road, but was originally the carriage drive within the grounds. The paddock gate probably opened on to this drive, and facing it was "the old house," on a site occupied now by a house of later date, which may contain some

HASTINGS' HOUSE, ALIPORE. NORTH VIEW.

HASTINGS' HOUSE, ALIPORE. SOUTH VIEW.

[*Face p.* 95.

portion or all of the old house built over. The bungalows would, of course, leave no trace when once pulled down, but the "large tank of excellent water" still remains.

"The description of the upper-roomed house in Lot 2 corresponds with the centre portion of Hastings House, which is all that existed in Hastings' time—the little house which seemed to Mrs. Fay a 'perfect bijou.' The stone staircase still stands, but can scarcely be called handsome, being narrow, winding, and steep. The back staircase is also in good preservation, it is built into an odd corner-cupboardlike wooden shaft, within a bath-room, and is lighted by a small-barred window which opens into the room. The Madras Chunam of the advertisement is lost under successive coats of whitewash.

"The hall and two rooms on each floor form the original house, the central block, while the wings are distinctly of a later period, as is evidenced by the style of the beams and burghas, and by the stucco work. The entire building is raised four feet from the ground, but only the wings are flued—another mark of the later period, and finally the walls of the wings do not 'bond' into those of the central block. This is very apparent on the southern front of the building."

In the same way as the surroundings of Hastings House are very different now to what they were ten years ago, so Hastings House of the above description was very different to what it has become since Lord Curzon rescued it from impending fate, and converted it into a state "guest-house" for Indian princes and nobles. At that time it had been vacant for many years, and stood forlorn and deserted, cut off from the outer world by its own spacious grounds, a melancholy spectacle of decay and desolation. Still more marked must have been the difference when the house was in the early days of its splendour: all that taste could suggest and wealth could supply had been lavished on its adornment, and the gracious presence of the brilliant Mrs. Hastings, the "beloved Marian" for whom this shrine had been prepared, shed a charm over all.

That Hastings House is the actual house in which Warren Hastings lived at Alipore is now indisputably proved, but that honour has repeatedly been claimed for "Belvedere." The mistake originated with Mrs. Fay, who, writing in 1780, spoke of Mrs. Hastings as residing at Belvedere House. Mrs. Fay was the wife of a barrister, and accompanied her husband to Calcutta in 1780, from where she wrote a series of lively, if not very accurate letters, to her relatives in England. More than thirty years later, when the writer had experienced trials and anxieties which, as she sadly complained, "had produced only a long train of blasted hopes and heart-rending disappointments," she published these early letters without apparently correcting her mistaken first impressions, and her statement that she had visited Mrs. Hastings at Belvedere House, about five miles from Calcutta, remained to puzzle and mislead successive generations of Calcutta residents.

Poor Mrs. Fay's "trials" began soon after her arrival in India, when she separated from her husband. Some years later, she, having in the mean time been home to England, returned to Calcutta with an "investment" of millinery and dresses, and two young ladies to assist her in disposing of her wares. She opened her shop in a house at the corner of Church Lane and Hastings Street, which overlooked the churchyard in the rear. This circumstance led to an entry in the Vestry records of St. John's Church, on the subject of a complaint by Mrs. Fay, regarding a boundary wall which shut out light and air from her lower rooms. In this record, dated 13th April, 1789, the house is alluded to as "formerly the Post Office," which gives us the origin of the name of "Old Post Office Street" directly opposite. The Post Office was probably removed from this house on account of its being reduced in size, as a portion of the building was pulled down about this period, when the erection of the church led to alterations in the neighbourhood, and Church Lane was widened by the addition of a strip of land taken from the old burial-ground. The house Mrs. Fay occupied, the "Old Post Office," still stands, and its windows overlooking the churchyard still lead to complaints, and disagreement with the Church authorities.

In Hastings Street, Mrs. Fay was a neighbour of her patroness Mrs. Hastings, whose "town house," which she had occupied in earlier years as Mrs. Imhoff, was at 7, Hastings Street, where some ancient punkahs, quaintly painted in crimson and gold, still remain, stranded waifs of the tide of fashion which once filled the old house with its flood.

But to return to Alipore and Belvedere. One of the earliest, if not the earliest mention of the house after Mrs. Fay's mistaken use of the name, is in the account of the duel between Hastings and Francis in August, 1780, when, after the encounter, the wounded Francis was carried to Belvedere, the house of Major Tolly, or Foley, as it has been erroneously read. Major Tolly was an engineer officer who obtained a grant of the Govindpore Creek, or Nullah, which

KIDDERPORE HOUSE IN 1794.

MRS. FAY'S HOUSE IN 1895.

[*Face p.* 98

authorized him to levy tolls on boats using the waterway, on condition that he deepened the channel and made it navigable. The grant was in the first instance for a period of twelve years, and it paid the enterprising officer sufficiently well for him to obtain an extension of the lease about 1780. He died, however, in 1784, and the Nullah appears to have been neglected and silted up, as in 1806 it was again considerably deepened and enlarged for a length of sixteen miles of its course. The Creek was held in great reverence by the Hindus, as it was believed to have been an old course of the sacred Ganges, in some far back period when the shrine of Kali was raised on its banks at Kalighat. Some idea of the condition of the Nullah in the early days of the English settlement may be formed, when we read that dying Hindus were laid on its muddy banks that their lives might ebb away amid the slime and ooze of the ebbing tide of the sacred stream, and their funeral pyres were lit on the spot where they breathed their last, the remains being cast into the venerated waters.

Other bodies which were cast into the canal and the river, without even a form of cremation, were those of those unfortunate convicts, and they were many, who died while undergoing their sentences. Even as late as 1811, an observer, who seems to have been more curious than shocked, wrote in reference to the convict hospital and the deaths there—

"Their transition is remarkably easy: they lie down to sleep and go off like the snuff of a candle. Their irons are not taken off till they are ascertained to be dead, when they are thrown into the Nullah—Mussulmans, I believe, as well as Hindus."

When Tolly bought "Belvedere," for the sake, no doubt, of its convenient situation as regards his canal, he probably did so from the Murshedabad family. During the Nawab Jaffir Ali's residence in Alipore, his family and retainers must have occupied a very large number of houses, forming quite a colony, as happened in the almost parallel case of the King of Oudh at Garden Reach, a century later, and it was probably one of these houses which Tolly bought and adapted to European requirements, and named it "Belvedere."

There were possibly several such houses in Belvedere grounds, which up to a much later date included the present gardens of the Agri-Horticultural Society. In these latter there stood, until recent years, the crumbling ruins of an old tomb which was known as the Begum's

Tomb, and was said to have been that of a member of the Murshedabad family. The tomb, which lies to the east of the tank at the entrance gate of the gardens, was levelled in 1890, and a handsome *Bougainvillea* trained over the spot to cover with its kindly veil, without disturbing, the unsightly remains.

Soon after the death of Colonel Tolly, as he had then become—in 1784, Belvedere was advertised for sale, but appears not to have found a purchaser, for in 1802 it was again advertised by order of the attorney to the administratrix of the late Colonel William Tolly. In this advertisement the property is described as "that large, commodious, and well-known house, called 'Belvidere House,'" and the rent, payable in London, was £350 yearly. Two other lots were also offered, comprising the land on each side of the road leading from Belvedere Bridge to Belvedere House, in the occupation of native tenants, and yielding a yearly rental of Rs. 600. When the house once more came into the market, which it did in 1809, it was described as "that superb mansion lately occupied by the commander-in-chief at the monthly rent of sicca rupees 450, and well-known as Belvedere House"—a detailed description of the nine rooms it contained is given; "also an elegant marble cold bath, and a hot bath," the whole "recently new matted."

"Belvedere" changed owners for the last time in 1854. It was then the property of Mr. Charles Prinsep, and was purchased from him by the Government to be the official residence of the Lieut.-Governors of Bengal. In Upjoin's map of 1794 the grounds of Belvedere are shown extending as far south as Belvedere Lane. Belvedere Road had not been made at that date, and the eastern boundary, which is now marked by that road, divided Belvedere grounds from those of "the Lodge," the garden house of Philip Francis, and now the residence of the Alipore magistrate. When the Government bought Belvedere the land had been divided, and a comparatively small portion went with the house. Some years later the remainder of the ground, one hundred biggahs, was offered for sale at a moderate price, but the Government declined to purchase; a little later it was put up for public sale, and a local butcher came forward as an intending purchaser of the land for grazing his stock. The mere suggestion of such a neighbour horrified the then Lieut.-Governor, and on his urgent representations the ground was purchased by Government at a considerable advance on the price asked before : forty biggahs were added to Belvedere, and the remaining sixty biggahs were subsequently made over to the Agricultural and Horticultural Society. At that time there was an old house on the ground, which was removed to make way for the Society's present building.

About the identity of the Alipore magistrate's house with the Lodge of Philip Francis, there is no question. When Francis owned it the house was a small lower-roomed dwelling, containing a hall and four rooms. The grounds were larger even than those of Belvedere, which bounded them on the west, and included the present jail, reformatory, and other buildings, the Nullah being the boundary on the other three sides. The entrance gate was near Belvedere, and the carriage drive, a portion of which is now the public road, remains unaltered to the present day. It was this house, in its splendid park, which Macrabie, Francis' brother-in-law, described as "pleasant to the last degree," and where choice spirits of Francis' acquaintance used to gather for a weekly symposium. Francis bought the property in 1775, about a year after his arrival in the country, and sold it for Rs. 30,000 in April, 1780, six months before he left India, to his friend Livius.

It is curious that Francis should not have

been taken to the Lodge rather than to Belvedere, after he had been wounded in the duel with Hastings, but no doubt the distance he would have had to be carried, round and through the extensive grounds of both houses, was the reason for taking him to that which was nearest. A detailed account of the duel was written by Colonel Peace, Hastings' second, in the form of a letter addressed to a friend at home, with the object of putting the exact circumstances on record, so that "if any reports different from what I have related should circulate, and you should think them worthy of contradiction, I hope you will not scruple to use this letter for that purpose." This account is sufficiently well known not to need quotation here, with the exception of the paragraph dealing with the exact locality. Colonel Pearce wrote—

"The place they were at was very improper for the business; it was the road leading to Allipore, at the crossing of it through a double row of trees, that formerly had been a walk of Belvidere garden on the western side of the house. Whilst Col. Watson went, by the desire of Mr. Francis, to fetch his pistols, that gentleman proposed to go aside from the road into the walk: but Mr. Hastings disapproved of the place because it was full of weeds and dark: the road itself was next mentioned, but was thought by everybody too public, as it was near riding time, and people might want to pass that way: it was therefore agreed to walk towards Mr. Barwell's house,* on an old road that separated his ground from Belvidere, and, before we had gone far, a retired dry spot was chosen as a proper place."

It will be noticed that Colonel Pearce wrote of "the road leading to Allipore" which implies that Belvedere was not included in Alipore, and that the name which may be taken as "the township of Ali" was applied, at that time, only to the group of the principal houses which had been occupied by Jaffir Ali. Hastings wrote repeatedly in his letters of his house as "Allypore Gardens," and the same name is used in the title-deeds of Hastings House, in one of which, dated 1806, the property is described as premises "known by the name of Allypore Gardens."

Colonel Pearce continued his description: "at the crossing of it through a double row of trees." The last survivors of a double row of trees, an avenue, still stand on the west side of the Alipore Road, opposite the west gate of Belvedere, and it is not a far-fetched

* Kidderpore House.

conjecture to suppose that these trees, which still border a road leading towards "Mr. Barwell's" Kidderpore House, mark the spot within a few yards where, on that damp and steamy August morning a century and a quarter ago, was fought the memorable duel which drove Philip Francis from the field in which he had schemed and plotted for power, and left Warren Hastings in a position to write, "After a conflict of six years, I may enjoy the triumph of a decided victory."

SIR PHILIP FRANCIS.

[*Face p.* 106.

CHAPTER VI

SOCIAL LIFE

Social manners and customs—Servants—Food—Wines—Hookahs—Carriages—Government House festivities—Rejoicings after Seringapatam—Clive's "bill" for earlier rejoicings, 1766—Court House gaieties—Balls.

SCATTERED up and down the pages of books of travel, and in the early numbers of the *Calcutta Review*, that delightful mine of information on Indian subjects both grave and gay, may be found pictures of English society in Calcutta from the earliest years of the settlement,—pictures which are curiously alike in their general outlines much as the details may vary, for all emphasize as characteristic the display of wealth, the craving for amusement, the enjoyment of the pleasures of the table, side by side with the courageous endurance of physical ills, the calm facing of Death in his most terrible aspects, the quiet prosecution of good works, from the "pious charity" which reared the first English Church of St. Anne and founded the

Charity School, to the distribution of rice on Surman's (Kidderpore) Bridge to the starving poor in years of famine. To the hospitality and generosity of Anglo-Indian society there is no lack of testimony. Lord Valentia, who was in Calcutta in 1803, and who subsequently published an account of his travels in the East, wrote :—

"I can truly affirm that my Eastern countrymen are hospitable in the highest degree, and that their generosity is unbounded. The hearts of the British in this country seem expanded with affluence, they do everything on a princely scale."

Again we read, in Forbes's "Oriental Memoirs" :—

"The character of the English in India is an honour to their country. In private life they are generous, kind, and hospitable; as husbands, fathers, masters, they cannot easily be excelled; whilst friendship, illustrated in its more general sense by unostentatious acts of humanity and benevolence, shines in India with conspicuous lustre. How often have the sons and daughters of misfortune experienced the blessed effects of Oriental benevolence! How often have the ruined merchant, the disconsolate widow, and the helpless orphan been relieved by the delicate and silent subscription, amounting in a few hours to several thousand pounds, without the child of sorrow knowing its benefactors!"

If the benevolence thus lauded was on a "princely scale," so also was the lavish hospitality—the balls, dinners, and breakfasts, when astonishing quantities of food and wine loaded the tables, and were consumed with appetite and zest. We have seen how in Captain Hamilton's time, in 1720, "the inhabitants of Calcutta" enjoyed a variety of fruit and fish and "all sorts of provisions both wild and tame." Sixty years later, Mrs. Fay, in one of her letters, discussed food supplies and prices, and gave a humorous picture of herself and her husband awaiting dinner. She wrote—

"We were frequently told in England, you know, that the heat in Bengal destroyed the appetite. I must own that I never yet saw any proof of that: on the contrary, I cannot help thinking that I never saw an equal quantity of victuals consumed. We dine, too, at two o'clock, in the very heat of the day. At this moment Mr. F. is looking out with a hawk's eye for his dinner, and, though still much of an invalid, I have no doubt of being able to pick a bit myself. I will give you our bill of fare, and the general prices of things: A soup, a roast fowl, curry and rice, a mutton pie, a forequarter of lamb, a rice pudding, tarts, very good cheese, fresh churned butter, fine bread, excellent Madeira (that is expensive, but eatables are very cheap). A whole sheep costs but two rupees, a lamb one rupee, six good fowls or ducks ditto, twelve pigeons ditto, twelve pounds of bread ditto, two pounds of butter ditto, and a joint of veal ditto."

In another letter, Mrs. Fay speaks of the highly spiced and seasoned dishes which were served at Calcutta tables, and describes particularly "Burdwan stew," a sort of "Hot-pot" in which fish, flesh, and fowl combined with unlimited seasoning, the whole prepared in a silver saucepan, resulted in the most appetizing of dishes. At this period, when dinner was at two o'clock, supper at ten o'clock was the next meal. Some years later, evening dinners between seven and eight o'clock were introduced; but as the midday meal was still retained under the name of *tiffin*, it is not surprising to find complaints of flagging appetite.

"Calcutta dinners are but a languid sort of things," wrote a visitor about 1805, "you have stomach perhaps to pick the bone of a floriken, or may get through a fine delicious snipe, but you cannot grapple with a slice of beef or of

Bengal mutton. The *tiffin*, a meal at two o'clock, defrauds the dinner of its homage due. But the luxury of the first glass of cool claret (*loll shraub*) that salutes your lips! Skilfully refrigerated, it is a celestial draught. The icy nectar courses down the whole system with the rapidity of lightning: the spirits are set free as from the torpor of enchantment, and the whole being undergoes a refreshing transformation."

The question of drinks has naturally always been one of first importance to Anglo-Indians, and claret stood first favourite though it had many rivals in public favour. But whatever the wine, it was essential it should be cold: this was effected by the use of saltpetre and Glauber's salts; and a special wine cooler, or *abdar*, was retained in every household, whose sole duty it was to keep the day's supply of "drinks" at the required temperature. Curiously enough, the earliest Anglo-Indians, the factors of Surat of the seventeenth century, favoured hot drinks rather than cold, and are said by Talboys Wheeler to have been the inventors of "punch," the name being corrupted from the Hindustani *panch*, five, derived from the five ingredients, spirits, lemon-juice, spices, sugar, and water, and he quotes Albert de Mandelslo, an early traveller, who visited Surat in 1638, who described it as—

"*palepuntz*, which is a kind of drink consisting of *aqua vitæ*, rose-water, juice of citrons, and sugar, of which some took more than they could well carry away. At our ordinary meeting every day we took only *thé*, which is commonly used all over India, not only among those of the country, but also among the Dutch and English, who take it as a drug that cleanses the stomach, and digests the superfluous humours by a temperate heart particular thereto."

This appreciation of tea is interesting from its early date, 1638, as tea did not reach England till 1650, and it was not till some years later, when the East India Company had presented King Charles II. with a gift of two pounds of tea, that it began to be better known, and to be drunk in fashionable circles. Another hot drink which the earlier factors favoured was "burnt wine," made by boiling wine with spices, which was drunk in the morning, as hot as could be sipped, to "comfort the stomach."

The difficulty and expense of importing European wines and brandy led to the use of the native spirit *arrack*, which was the cause of an immense deal of drunkenness and terrible mortality, especially among the young writers and soldiers. The high prices of wine, which varied considerably according to the quantity in the market, were no bar however to the wealthy members of society, and it was usual for a man to take his three bottles of claret after dinner daily, besides the Madeira which he consumed during the meal, and for a lady to drink one bottle of wine a day. Much of this wine had to be taken perforce, as it were, in honouring the many toasts which it was customary to propose; at public dinners, tiffins, and breakfasts there were never less than ten, and often over twenty-five toasts on the lists. At private tables etiquette required that the host and hostess should take wine with each guest, and every guest should do the same with each one present; and when all toasts and healths had been duly honoured, there would still be a few "sentiments" left to wind up with.

It is not a little surprising that people should have had the spirit and strength to be so sociable and convivial, when we remember that the houses in which they lived, in spite of spacious and lofty rooms and wide gardens, were sadly lacking in much that is deemed indispensable by Anglo-Indians of the present day to ameliorate the conditions of the climate. When Lord Teignmouth first arrived in Bengal, in 1769, he described Calcutta as consisting of houses "not two or three of which were furnished with venetian blinds or glass windows, solid shutters being generally used, and rattans like those used for the bottoms of chairs, in lieu of panes, whilst little provision was made against the heat of the climate." We may conclude that Hastings House, more than ten years later, was without glazed windows, since Mrs. Fay was unable to see what the gardens were like, the house being "hermetically closed" against the heat. Even in dress very little concession was made to the climate: the men wore white jackets and, even sometimes in later years, white trousers, as dinner dress in place of black broadcloth; but wigs and powdered hair were worn by all, and men swathed their throats with voluminous neckcloths, and ladies crowned their elaborate *coiffure* with heavy turbans to attend a crowded reception, or to dance till daybreak at a ball, even in the sultry month of May.

Dancing was always a favourite amusement in Calcutta, and the ladies being in the minority did their best to redress the balance by each dancing as many dances as she could possibly crowd into one night. One writer described Calcutta ladies as dancing from nine in the

THE COUNCIL HOUSE AND ESPLANADE, 1792.

[*Face p.* 114.

evening till five o'clock in the morning; and Lord Valentia, who took everything very seriously, wrote—

"Consumptions are very frequent among the ladies, which I attribute in a great measure to their incessant dancing, even during the hottest weather. After such violent exercise they go into the verandahs, and expose themselves to a cool breeze and damp atmosphere."

Much of this dancing took place in the Old Court House, which for over thirty years was the scene of most of the public entertainments, and assembly balls. Towards the close of the century the old house became unsafe; society, too, had begun to break up into classes, and subscription assemblies went out of fashion. Entertainments of every kind were transferred to private houses, and hosts, led by the Governor-General in his new and splendid Government House, gave weekly receptions, besides large dinner-parties, balls, and *fêtes*.

The eventful years at the close of the eighteenth and beginning of the nineteenth century gave many opportunities for entertainments, and other displays of rejoicing, either for victories obtained in war, or for the return of peace, or the celebration of some important treaty. A curious document in connection with one of these occasions is "Lord Clive's bill of 1st January, 1766," which was passed and paid in the Proceedings of the Calcutta Board in February of the same year. Clive had concluded a treaty with Shuja-ul-Dowlah, Nawab Vizier of Oude, by which the East India Company obtained the *Dewanny* of the three provinces of Bengal, Behar, and Orissa, and his bill of expenses ran as follows:—

	Rs.	An.	Pies.
Charges for building and fitting up an assembly house with furniture for celebrating the late peace concluded with Shuja-ul-Dowlah .	4,853	7	3
Expense of feeding wild beasts and making a place for them to fight in	384	14	3
Charges paid for fireworks on this occasion . .	12,179	8	0
Sundry presents to the keepers of the wild beasts, etc.	2,426	15	3
Expenses of three public entertainments . .	3,927	2	6
Paid for liquors	5,451	9	0
	29,223	8	3

This celebration took place in Oude, and had more of the character of native rejoicings. In Calcutta "wild beasts" formed no part of any of the entertainments, in which, however, fireworks were generally introduced as a show which could be enjoyed by the populace at large. The *Calcutta Gazette* of January, 1803, gave a detailed account of the elaborate illuminations and fireworks which formed part of a grand *fête*, the first public entertainment held in Government House, which was given by Lord Wellesley in honour of "the Peace." The evening opened with a ball, at which there were present some eight hundred guests, including the chief justice and judges of the Supreme Court, the members of Council, several natives of rank and position, the Danish Governor of Serampore, and Lord Valentia, who had only landed in Calcutta the same day after a voyage of seven months from England. Lord Wellesley, who was at the time residing in "the Treasury" pending the completion of Government House, dined with the town major, Major Calcraft, in the Fort, from where he drove to the "new Government House" about ten o'clock. Soon after he entered the ballroom, dancing commenced, and continued till twelve o'clock, when the company proceeded to supper in the marble hall, where six ranges of tables "were covered with a profusion of every delicacy," says the chronicler of the *Calcutta Gazette*, "and were ornamented in a style of superior taste and magnificence." We can form some idea of these table decorations when we read—

"The most remarkable objects were a galley bringing the intelligence of the Peace: a frigate decorated with colours: some curious Egyptian obelisks covered with hieroglyphics, and a temple emblematical of the Peace, and of the gallant exploits of our Naval and Military Commanders during the late war. The temple consisted of eight Corinthian pillars supporting four pediments, the whole crowned by a light dome. The pediments were ornamented with paintings of the action off Cape St. Vincent, 14th February, 1798; the Battle of the Nile, 1st August, 1798; the storming of Seringapatam, 4th May, 1799; and the landing of the British Army in Egypt on the 8th of March, 1801; while the friezes bore appropriate mottoes with the names of distinguished soldiers, sailors, and statesmen."

From supper the company were summoned by the discharge of a rocket at one o'clock, to view the illuminations and fireworks, "which were executed by artificers sent to Calcutta for the purpose from Lucknow and Murshedabad." Lord Valentia wrote rather disparagingly of the illuminations: "The populace stole much of the oil, and as it was impossible to light so great a range at one time the effect was inferior to what it ought to have been," but the rockets which were discharged from mortars on the Fort ramparts he considered superior to any he had ever beheld. The *Calcutta Gazette* account, however, had nothing but praise for all, and dwelt with evident enjoyment on every detail. It thus describes the elaborate display :—

"Opposite the southern front of the Government House was an illuminated façade, forty feet high, extending three hundred and fifty feet on each side of a temple dedicated to Peace, in the lower part of which was a transparent painting, fifteen feet square, 'Britannia destroying the implements of War, and receiving the olive branch from Peace.' On one side the temple of Janus shut: on the other the ocean, ships sailing, etc. The Royal Arms were displayed in the pediment. A range of double pilastres of the Doric order led to the temples of Fame and Valour, in the intervals of which portraits of eminent statemen, and highly distinguished officers were displayed. From the temples of Valour and Fame a chain of illuminations, rising in pyramidical forms thirty-six feet in height, was continued to the Dhurrumtolla on the left, and to Chandpaul Ghaut on the right. Opposite to each wing of the Government House were three lofty and illuminated arches (the arch in the centre rising sixty feet), crowned with appropriate ornaments."

On the east front of Government House a transparency represented a battle, "Lake," in a wreath of laurel, on the top. On the west front another transparency showed a view of Seringapatam, with portraits of Generals Harris and

Baird, and appropriate emblems; and on the northern front was a transparency forty feet high —"Britannia supporting the world to which she has restored Peace." Arabesque scrolls of light connected the whole in one continued illumination, comprehending an extent of near three miles.

Among the most remarkable objects in the fireworks were four figures of fire representing the fight of elephants, admirably conducted, and an ingenious device of a globe, which, after discharging fire for some time, opened, and discovered a transparency in Persian characters to the following effect: "May your Prosperity be perpetual."

This grand ball, the first of the long series of splendid entertainments which Government House has seen since that day, was followed a few months later by a public breakfast, on the anniversary of the fall of Seringapatam, the 4th of May. The company assembled at half-past eight o'clock, and were conducted to the breakfast tables prepared in the centre and south rooms of the marble floor, the columns of which were beautifully ornamented with a variety of flowers corresponding with the ornaments of the tables, which were also decorated with various emblems in the form of columns, temples, and trophies, "commemorating the principal political and military events which contributed to the fall of the hostile power of Mysore, and to the final restoration of peace in India." The breakfast was followed by a levee from half-past nine to half-past ten o'clock.

Another grand entertainment, which took place in this same month of May, 1803, was a concert, ball, and supper given by the gentlemen of the settlement to the Marquis of Wellesley, "to commemorate the various brilliant events of His Excellency's Administration," which took place in the "New College." This building stood on the south side of Dalhousie Square, and was known to many generations of Calcutta citizens as the "Exchange;" it was rented by Lord Wellesley when he planned his splendid scheme for the Wellesley College, as a temporary home for the college till a suitable building could be erected at Garden Reach. To the deep mortification of the Governor-General, the Court of Directors peremptorily refused to sanction his proposal, but this was not till a twelve-month after it had been put forward, and "the Exchange" continued for some time to be known by the name of the New College.

The entertainment, as befitted the gentlemen of the settlement and their distinguished guest, was on the most lavish scale. We read of ceilings and columns beautifully decorated with artificial flowers, numerous large mirrors which reflected the brilliant lights of a beautiful display of lustres and girandoles, a superb canopy containing a splendid punkah over a gilt chair of state for the reception of His Excellency, a grand orchestra; and everywhere on ceilings, walls, columns, orchestra, and standards blazed the star and the tiger-stripe of Tippoo Sultan in commemoration of the Conquest of Mysore. The allusion was repeated in the rose-coloured sashes and bandeaux of the four hundred servants in attendance, and even appeared in the rich dresses of the ladies. One of these is thus described:—

"The dress was white muslin of gold spangles, and richly embroidered round the bottom of the gown and sleeves with a border composed of the tiger-stripe and star alternate in purple and gold: this device was copied from the colours of Tippoo Sultan taken at Seringapatam. The head-dress was a white spangled turban, with ornaments similar to the border of the gown, and decorated with a plume of white feathers."

This striking dress was apparently worn by several ladies, possibly those who took part in the concert, in which there appears to have been only one soloist, a Mr. Du Sart, who sang some complimentary stanzas in French, and "a grand song in honour of the capture of Seringapatam, the words of which were composed on the occasion by an amateur of this settlement." No other names are given in the account in the *Calcutta Gazette*, but—

"two glees, and the charming duett of 'Piche Cornahie' excited general applause, and the concert was concluded by the March in 'Judas Maccabæus,' and Handel's celebrated and (on this occasion) appropriate chorus of—

> 'Sing unto God, and high affections raise
> To crown this conquest with unmeasured praise.'

which was performed by the boys belonging to the church, and by all the amateurs of Calcutta, and was deservedly encored."

At a time when it took a full year to obtain any article from England, and shops were not, it must have been a difficult problem for the members of this gay society to keep a wardrobe supplied. In those days, too, a man's dress was as elaborate an affair as a lady's, and required lace and ruffles, ribbon and powder, buckles and brooches, to say nothing of "black and white hats, thunder and lightning coats, stockings of seven colours, and tamboured waistcoats bedaubed with flowers," so that it was surely a triumph of foresight and taste as well as wealth that there appears to have been no lack of rich toilettes; and no account of ball or masquerade, dinner or breakfast, or other entertainment seems to have been complete without a more or less detailed reference to the dresses of the ladies and their cavaliers. The demand for wearing apparel soon created a source of supply; enterprising stewards and stewardesses of the ships, and even the captains themselves, took to bringing out "investments" of clothing and household goods. The arrival and date of sale of these investments were notified to all residents, at first by a messenger who carried the notice from house to house, in later days by an advertisement in the *Calcutta Gazette*, which brought fashionable society flocking to the sale-room. One of these advertisements is a fair sample of all:—

"Thursday, July 15, 1784. Fresh Europe goods for sale. Messrs. Baxter and Ord most respectfully beg leave to inform the Ladies and Gentlemen they have purchased the investment of Captain Johnson of the *Berrington*, consisting of the following elegant assortment of goods, which are of the latest fashions, and the highest perfection, having left England so late as February last."

The list which follows begins with an elegant assortment of millinery and "Piano-Fortes with organs underneath and Flute stops," and ranges from mahogany furniture, wines, ale, cheese, pickles, and herrings, ladies hats with feathers, gentlemen's ditto, and children's ditto, boots and shoes, fancy cloths, doe breeches, and gloves, to vinegar, oil, and mustard, guns and telescopes, books and "perambulators," spectacles and speaking-trumpets. This varied assortment of goods were to be sold at low prices, with a deduction of ten per cent. for cash paid on delivery, and eight per cent. for all bills paid at the end of the month.

As this trade became established, other and more ambitious rivals entered the field. Mrs. Fay, as we have seen, opened a shop in 1785, and imported two young ladies to assist her in it; and many others came and went several times between London and Calcutta with their investments, a speculation of no little enterprise, considering that the voyage each way occupied six months, and was liable to risks of shipwreck, piracy, and foreign capture. Mrs. Fay herself, when on her first voyage to Bengal, was with her husband made prisoner by Hyder Ali, and only reached Calcutta after suffering many hardships. When Sir Elijah Impey left India in 1783 with his wife and children, his ship, the *Worcester*, sprang a leak, the captain died, and the vessel narrowly escaped being wrecked on St. Helena, where the party landed, and paid one thousand pounds for a passage in the *Dutton* for the remainder of their journey. Those were the days when the captains of homeward-bound Indiamen demanded, and received, eight thousand rupees, or one thousand pounds for the passage of a single person, and fifteen hundred pounds for a married couple.

Divided from the home country by such tremendous obstacles, India was literally a land of exile to the Englishmen and women who dwelt there, and they seem to have done their best to gild their cage, and to compensate themselves for the loss of Western comfort, by indulgence in Eastern splendour. A curious old Anglo-Indian novel, called "The Baboo," gave a description of the forms and ceremonies surrounding the domestic life of a high official and his wife in Calcutta, in the early years of the nineteenth century. A typical scene presented the lady descending from her room in the studied *negligé* of a fashionable morning toilette, and passing to the breakfast table through the marshalled ranks of her retinue of servants all bowing low as she passed. These

CHOWRINGHEE FROM THE MAIDAN, 1792.

[*Face p.* 126.

numerous servants were a striking feature in Anglo-Indian life, as they are to this day, although their numbers have dwindled considerably. An establishment of the old days, besides a complement of table servants, bearers, cook and cook's mates, included such dignitaries as a *chobdar*, or mace-bearer (silver stick in waiting), whose duty it was to marshal the procession when his master took his walks abroad or rode in his palanquin. Even when carriages had superseded palanquins, this functionary remained an ornamental appendage to every household of consequence. Then there were the *jemadar* and his *peons* or *chupprassies*, who formed a body-guard; the *palkee-bearers*, who cost thirty rupees a month; the *mussalchees*, now degenerated to a race of scullions, but once, as their name denotes, torch-bearers, who ran swiftly, "at the rate of full eight miles an hour," with blazing torches before their masters' carriages, to light them safely on their way. Still other servants were the *barber*, whose services received the modest pay of two to four rupees, and the *hairdresser*, whose artistic skill was recognized in a salary of sixteen rupees a month; the *abdar*, who cooled the wines; the *hookabardar*, who had sole charge of the master's, and very often the mistress's, *hookah*—the Indian pipe, which no other hand than his might touch. Very skilfully did the *hookabardar* prepare the rich, soft, brown mass of tobacco, in which were cunningly mingled fragrant spices, luscious treacle—rich, and pure from the cane presses,—and cool rose-water. When the master dined abroad, his *hookabardar* accompanied him with the precious *hooka*, the *khansamah* came to wait on him at table, and the *bearer*, carrying a cool, white jacket, to replace the regulation broadcloth in which the guest must present himself to his host. Dinner over, and the wine on the table, the *hookabardars* would file in, each to lay beside his master's chair a small square of carpet, on which the *hookah* stood in all its bravery of chased silver stand and cover, with graceful drooping silver chains, and long bright silken snake which carried forward to the smoker's hand the handsome silver mouth-piece delicately scented with rose-water. Then would rise the fragrant smoke from the glowing discs of prepared charcoal, the soft gurgling of the water filled the pauses in the conversation, and Nicotine in fairest form held soothing sway.

CHAPTER VII

THE CHURCHES

St. John's Church—Fashions at Church—Palanquins—Carriages—St. Paul's Cathedral—Zoffany's picture at St. John's and at Brentford—Begum Johnson and her history.

WHEN the British recovered Calcutta from Suraj-ud-Dowlah's forces, in 1757, they found the English portion of the town in a deplorable state of ruin, none of the buildings within and around the Fort having escaped the destructive hands of the Mussulman soldiery. The church, which had stood for over forty years nearly opposite the main gate of the Fort, was a heap of ruins. It had been utilized by the besieged and besiegers in turn, during the attack on Calcutta, and had suffered considerably, and at the last it had been fired with other buildings, and was so absolutely destroyed that there could be no thought of building a new church on the desecrated site. During the first decade after the return of the British to the town, all their resources and energies, as regards building, were devoted to the new Fort and to dwelling-houses. Not only had most of the former houses been destroyed, but the number of Europeans requiring accommodation had greatly increased, owing to the large number of military officers who had come with the troops from Madras. The junior officers and young writers had to manage as best they could in slight "apartments" of mat and thatch, while the seniors fared but little better in badly patched houses, both building materials and builders being scarce. Even in 1768 it was said that, though the town of Calcutta was daily increasing in size, "the English inhabitants multiply so fast that houses are extremely scarce." Under these circumstances it was natural that the building of a church should be relegated to the distant future, when the new Fort should have been completed, and that, in the mean while, the chaplain had to find what place he could for the celebration of Divine Service. The banishment of the Romish priests from the settlement for a time, allowed him the use of their chapel—a "damp and unwholesome" little brick building, on the site of the Moorgehatta Cathedral; but in 1760 this chapel was restored to its rightful owners, and a room, which cost Rs. 2,500, was built by the main gate of the Old Fort for use as a chapel, as a temporary measure, till a

ST. JOHN'S CHURCH. 1794.

[Face p. 131.

new presidency church could be built within the new Fort. The worthy Directors of the East India Company were very particular as to the due attendance of their covenanted and military officers at church, and had standing orders on the subject, besides giving the Calcutta Board occasional reminders that their servants "be required to give due obedience thereto." This ensured a regular congregation, and all Calcutta society met regularly at church on Sunday mornings, for there was no evening service: where also young ladies, on their first arrival in the settlement, made their public *début*. The lively writer of "Hartly House, Calcutta," a collection of letters published in 1789, gave an account of a quaint custom permitted on such occasions:—

"I have been at church, my dear girl," she wrote, "in my new palanquin (the model of genteel conveyance), where all ladies are approached, by sanction of ancient custom, by *all* gentlemen indiscriminately, known or unknown, with offers of their hand to conduct them to their seat. Accordingly those gentlemen who wish to change their condition (which, between ourselves, are chiefly old fellows), on hearing of a ship's arrival make a point of repairing to this holy dome, and eagerly tender their services to the fair strangers, who, if this stolen view happens to captivate, often, without undergoing the ceremony of a formal introduction, receive matrimonial overtures."

This picture is, no doubt, slightly overdrawn, but it is easy to see how such a custom must have arisen when we remember that that "model of genteel conveyance," the palanquin, conveyed only a single person, and the lady's natural escort could not be in attendance to assist her to, not alight, but rise from her conveyance when it had been deposited on the ground.

The palanquin of old times was very different from the ugly boxlike modern palkee. Surgeon Ives described it as "a covered machine with cushions in it, arched in the middle to give more room and air, and carried on the shoulders of four or six men." Tavernier, the enterprising and observant merchant-traveller of the seventeenth century, gave a more interesting and minute description of the genuine Indian palanquin, which, with possibly slight alterations, was the same as that used by the English.

"The *pallankeen*," wrote the Frenchman, "is a kind of bed of six or seven feet long, and three feet wide, with a small rail all round. A sort of cane, called bamboo, which they bend when young in order to cause it to take the form of a bow, in the middle sustains the cover of the *pallankeen*, which is of satin or brocade; and when the sun shines on one side, an attendant, who walks near the *pallankeen*, takes care to lower the covering. There is another, who carries at the end of a stick a kind of basket-work shield, covered with some sort of beautiful stuff, in order to promptly shelter the occupant of the *pallankeen* from the heat of the sun when it turns and strikes him on the face. The two ends of the bamboo are attached on both sides to the body of the *pallankeen*, between two poles joined together in a *saltier*, or St. Andrew's cross; and each of these poles is five or six feet long. Three men at most place themselves at each of these two ends, to carry the *pallankeen* on the shoulder, the one on the right, the other on the left, and they travel in this way faster than our chairmen in Paris, and with an easier pace, being trained to the trade from an early age."

This was the sort of palanquin which was considered by the East India Company to be a "piece of eastern luxury," in which they forbid their junior servants to indulge; and Ives records that they—[1]

"gave the strictest orders that none of these young gentlemen should be allowed even to hire a *roundel*-boy, whose business it is to walk by his master and defend him with his *roundel*, or umbrella, from the sun. A young fellow of humour, on this last order coming out, altered the form of his umbrella from a round to a square, called it a *squaredel* instead of a *roundel*, and insisted, that no order yet in force forbade him the use of it."

However grand and luxurious its outward appearance, the palanquin had many drawbacks: To get into it, it was necessary to enter backwards—a feat which men performed standing, the bearers lowering the poles from the shoulder to the fore-arm. As ladies' skirts forbade such a display of athletics on their part, the palanquin would be placed on the ground, from which it was raised some three or four inches by the legs on which it stood. The intending occupant would sit into it, and then gather up her skirts and feet, and turn inwards—a process sadly detrimental, one would think, to a fashionable toilette, and a performance in which it must have been difficult, for even the young and slender, to display either grace or dignity.

At a later period palanquins, or palkees, as they came to be called, were closed in with a roof and sides, with sliding-panel doors in place of the awning and draperies. They were upholstered like carriages, and painted and varnished in the same style. Sedan chairs were also introduced from England; and the *tonjon*, a chair with movable hood, became popular at one time, and was used by Lady William Bentinck during her stay in India, when her husband was Governor-General, from 1828 to 1835.

Before the sack of Calcutta there were but few carriages in the settlement, but as the town began to spread, and roads were made, the number of conveyances increased. M. Grandpré, writing in 1790, said that Calcutta, exclusive of palanquins,—

"abounds with all sorts of carriages, chariots, whiskies, and phaetons, which occasion in the evening as great a bustle as in one of the principal towns of Europe. There are also a great number of saddle horses, some of the Persian breed of exquisite beauty, but not Arabians, except a small sort called *pooni*, which are very much in vogue for phaetons."

It is supposed that the word "whiskies," used in the above account as the name of a carriage, is a mistake, and should be "britzska," a term which is now as obsolete as, and conveys even less meaning to the modern ear than "whiskies," which at least suggests being whisked along at a rapid rate! Besides the britzska, which was at one time a very fashionable conveyance, and was something between a barouche and a phaeton, there have been a variety of names for different styles of conveyance which have been in fashion at different times. The writer of an article in the *Calcutta Review*, in 1844, drew a series of comparisons between Calcutta as it was in his day, and as it had been fifty years earlier; and, with much complacency and pride, enumerated the variety of carriages to be seen in the town —"britzskas, barouches, landaulets, chariots, phaetons, buggies, palanquins, palki-gharries, brownberries, and crahanchys."

A great deal of emulation and rivalry used to be shown in the decoration and appointments of these fine carriages, and the chariots especially were very gorgeous affairs, with their great springs, and deep bodies, the handsome hammer-cloth, and silver-mounted harness: the coachman, in flat disc-like turban, with crested band across, and full *cummerbund*, or waist-cloth; and the running footmen with their *chowries*, or fly-whisks of great yaks' tails, mounted on silver handles, slung across the shoulder. A handsome carriage of her own was the ambition of every young lady of proper spirit, which led to a bachelor's fine equipage being called a "wife-trap" by the wits of the day. An amusing story in this connection is given in the *Calcutta Gazette* of the

ST. JOHN'S CHURCH, 1905.

[*Face p.* 137.

15th of March, 1787, under the heading of *Bon-Mot* :—

"A gentleman, remarkable for his gallantry and elegance of his equipage, drove up to a young lady, a night or two ago, on the course, and, after a little conversation, asked how she liked his wife-trap. 'Very well, sir; I think it a very handsome carriage.' 'And pray, madam, how do you like the bait within side?' 'Pray, sir,' replied the lady, "do you speak in French or English?"

In spite of the carriages, the palanquin continued to hold its own till well into the nineteenth century. St. John's Church had not been built very long, when it was found necessary to provide special slopes for the palkees to approach the entrance, where the riders might alight apart from the dust and inconvenience of the carriageway, and a palkee-shed was built on the south side of the churchyard, where they might remain sheltered from sun and rain while service was proceeding.

St. John's Church was consecrated in 1787. After having been talked of for years, the scheme for building a new presidency church took shape in December, 1783, when a public meeting was held, and a committee headed by the Governor-General, Warren Hastings, was appointed to receive subscriptions, which amounted to no less a sum than Rs. 35,950 on the first day, and totalled over a hundred and seventy thousand rupees by the time the church was completed. The ground selected for building the church was the old Powder Magazine Yard, which adjoined the burial-ground on the east. This plot of land had been sold by the Government to the Maharaja Nob-kissen, who now conveyed it back to Warren Hastings for the purpose of building a church. In the end, however, this ground was not utilized for the actual building, but formed the churchyard on the east, while the church was erected entirely within the boundaries of the old burial-ground, and the foundations were laid among the mouldering remains of scores upon scores of those who had died during the ninety years of the English occupation.

The church was erected from the design of Lieutenant James Agg, and under his superintendence; and chunar stone was largely used in its construction, as well as stone from the ruins of Gour, from where it was also proposed at first, but not carried out, to bring coloured marbles from the tombs of the old kings of Bengal. The stone church, or *Pathuriya Girja* as the natives call it, was consecrated on the 24th of June, 1787, under the name of St. John, and remained the presidency church till 1814, when, Calcutta having been constituted a bishopric, St. John's became

ST. PAUL'S CATHEDRAL

[Face p. 139.

the Cathedral. Old St. James's Church was built in 1820, the Free School Church, St. Thomas's, in 1831, and St. Peter's, in the Fort, in 1835, but it was not till 1839 that, it having been found impracticable to enlarge St. John's Church to meet the growing needs of the community, the scheme for building a new Cathedral took definite form. The Government gave a site in Chowringhee: Bishop Wilson, to whose strenuous efforts the success of the scheme was due, gave two lakhs of rupees: three lakhs of rupees were raised by public subscription and donations from the great missionary societies. In October, 1839, the foundation-stone was laid; and in October, 1847, St. Paul's Cathedral was consecrated; and St. John's Church fell back from its leading position, retaining only the name of the "Old Cathedral," by which it is known to many even at the present day.

Among the many munificent gifts to St. Paul's Cathedral, were a superb set of silver-gilt plate for the service of the Holy Communion, from Queen Victoria; and a painting of the Crucifixion by West and Forrest, which, with Her Majesty's sanction, was presented by the Dean and Canons of Windsor. This picture was one of three, which were designed by West, in 1787, for the western windows of St. George's Chapel, Windsor, when King George III. was restoring that edifice. The painting is described as "a representation of the Crucifixion, including the two thieves, angels flying above, and the heads and shoulders of Roman soldiers seen below."

It was found that the insertion of these windows at the western end of St. George's Chapel would involve, as in the case of the eastern window, the removal of all the stone work and tracery, except the two main mullions; and as this was strongly objected to, the intention was abandoned.

The two paintings for the aisles were finished, and inserted; but that for the central window, of which only the main group had been completed at the time of Forrest's death, remained in its unfinished state in the Chapter House at Windsor till, in 1847, it was presented to the Bishop of Calcutta for his new Cathedral. Here it was placed in the eastern window—a position which it occupied till it fell in the great cyclone of 1864, when it was replaced by one erected by public subscription. The windows on either side were given at a much later period by the Government of India—the one in memory of Bishop Milman, and the other to the memory of Lord Mayo, the latter from a design by Burne-Jones.

It may be noted in passing, that when, in 1790, West's altar-piece was placed in position in

ZOFFANY'S PICTURE—ST. JOHN'S CHURCH, CALCUTTA.

[*Face p.* 141.

St. George's Chapel, Windsor, it displaced one that had occupied the same place at the time of the Great Rebellion. This latter picture, a "Representation of the Last Supper," had been brought back to the altar in 1702, and remained there until superseded by West's picture, when it was given to Windsor parish church, where it is at the present time. West's picture, superseded in its turn in 1863, is now in the east aisle of St. George's Chapel.

It was at the time that the future President of the Royal Academy was painting the altar-piece for St. George's Chapel, that another Royal Academician, Zoffany, painted, in Calcutta, a picture, "The Last Supper," which he, in 1787, presented for an altar-piece to St. John's Church, then approaching completion.

John Zoffany was one of the earliest Royal Academicians. He was obliged to leave England, owing, it is said, to the ill feeling he had roused against himself through his injudicious indulgence in the habit of introducing the portraits of his friends and acquaintances into his pictures without the permission of the original, and often in unflattering guise. He arrived in India about the year 1781, and spent some years in Lucknow, where he amassed a considerable fortune by painting the portraits of members of the native nobility. In 1787, Zoffany was residing in Calcutta; his name is given in the list of professions in an almanac for that year, under the heading "Artist and portrait painter." The *Calcutta Gazette*, for April 12, 1787, announced—

"We hear Mr. Zoffany is employed in painting a large historical picture, 'The Last Supper:' he has already made considerable progress in the work, which promises to equal any production which has yet appeared from the pencil of this able artist, and, with that spirit of liberality for which he has ever been distinguished, we understand he means to present it to the public as an altar-piece for the New Church."

The building committee of the church accepted the painter's offer with enthusiasm, and were anxious to present him with a return gift of a ring of five thousand rupees value; but they found the funds at their disposal did not admit of the outlay, and were therefore obliged to content themselves by sending the artist a handsome letter of thanks. When the church was consecrated the painting had been finished and hung in its place, and must have caused no small sensation in Calcutta society when it was found that the figures in the picture were more or less faithful likenesses of members of the community.

The three principal figures in the picture, the Saviour, St. John, and Judas Iscariot, were portraits. The original of the first is said to have been a Greek priest, Father Parthenio, who was well known in Calcutta for his piety and good works. St. John was represented by Mr. Blaquiere, who was for years a magistrate of Calcutta; and in Judas Iscariot was pilloried an old resident of the town, Tulloh, the auctioneer. The remaining figures appear to have been less exact portraits, and the names of others who appeared in the canvas have not come down to the present day.

There can be little doubt that Calcutta society was considerably scandalized by the painter's curious humour, but he seems to have been very well satisfied with his efforts, for ten years later he repeated the performance in England. Again he painted a picture of the Last Supper, again he took his friends and neighbours for his models, and again presented the work to a church for an altar-piece. He was then living at Strand-on-the-Green, near Kew and Brentford, and it is said that he painted the picture for the parish church of the former place, but, as the authorities refused to pay as high a price as he demanded, he declined to let them have it, and made a gift of the painting to Brentford, where it may still be seen in St. George's Church. In this picture, Zoffany himself figures as St. Peter, a strong full face with small grey beard; and the face of St. John is a portrait of the painter's young wife; whom he married on his return from abroad. The Apostles were painted from local fishermen, and a curious proof that the figures were actual portraits was the fact that the grandson of one of the men, whose likeness has thus been preserved, was so exactly like his grandsire that he might well have been taken for the original of the figure in the canvas.

The two pictures do not agree in their arrangement. In the foreground of the St. John's painting are shown a great laver of brass with a ewer and small dish, while in the Brentford picture their place is occupied by two figures, who appear to be about to descend from the "large upper room" by steps, to which access is given by an opening in the floor. The figures are those of a white youth and a negro, the latter a portrait of the artist's "black slave." It is thought that Zoffany, by the introduction of these two figures, the negro and the Caucasian, in connection with the Jewish type, wished to exemplify the three races of mankind—the descendants of Shem, Ham, and Japhet, sharers alike in the blessing of the New Dispensation.

ZOFFANY'S PICTURE—ST. GEORGE'S CHURCH, BRENTFORD.

[*Face p.* 144.

To return to St. John's Church, Calcutta, in the days while it was still the "New Church." By a curious arrangement the galleries of the church were reserved for the leading officials and their ladies, while the floor of the building was left for subordinates and their families, and the poor members of the community. Even more curious was the arrangement by which the ladies and gentlemen sat apart. In the centre of the northern gallery were the seats of the Governor-General and his Council, and behind them were arrayed the ladies of the settlement. In the southern gallery, facing the Governor and Council, sat the judges of the Supreme Court, and with them sat the gentlemen; while in the western gallery, flanking the organ and choir, were the respective pews of the churchwardens' and the chaplain's families.

In this latter pew sat, at the time the church was consecrated, a very notable personage—the lady of Chaplain William Johnson, known to more than one generation of Calcutta residents as Begum Johnson. It was in a great measure due to the sustained efforts of Mr. Johnson that the erection of the church was undertaken and carried through, but, beyond the fact that he was an ardent Freemason, there seems little to record of him of interest, save that he was the fourth husband of "the Begum."

Mrs. Johnson's tomb, in excellent preservation, is in St. John's Churchyard, and her epitaph records her history at length. She was Frances, second daughter of Edward Crook, Esq., Governor of Fort St. David, an English factory on the Madras coast, near the French settlement of Pondicherry. Her father declined the post of Governor of Fort St. George (Madras), on account of his "age and infirm health," and retired to England, but it does not appear whether his family accompanied him. When Frances was in her twentieth year, she married, in Calcutta, the nephew of the then Governor (Mr. Braddyll), Parry Purple Templer, Esq. The date of this marriage is given in the epitaph as 1738, but the Rev. Mr. Hyde has been able to prove by the old parish registers that the correct date is November 3, 1744. Exactly four years later, on the 2nd of November, 1748, the young wife, who had then been a widow for nine months, was married to her second husband, James Althen, Esq.; and ten days later he died of smallpox, and she was once more a widow. When November came round again, the doubly-widowed Frances, who was still under twenty-five, stood once again before the altar in St. Anne's, and became the wife of William Watts, Esq., Senior Member of the Council in Bengal.

When the Nawab Aliverdi Khan died, in 1756, and was succeeded by his grandson, Suraj-ud-Dowlah, Mr. Watts was chief of the Company's factory at Cossimbazar, near Murshedabad; and when the young nawab plundered the factory, Mr. and Mrs. Watts with their three children were taken to Murshedabad, where Mr. Watts was placed in strict confinement, while his wife and children, two girls and a boy, were taken under the protection of the begum, the widow of Aliverdi Khan, and grandmother of Suraj-ud-Dowlah. Mrs. Watts had, no doubt, been on terms of friendship with the begum during the lifetime of the old nawab: she now received every care and attention from her friend, who, while the nawab was still in the neighbourhood of Calcutta, sent the mother and children under a strong escort to Chandernagore, where they were hospitably received and entertained by the French authorities. Mr. Watts had in the mean time been sent to Hughly, where he and other English prisoners were released by the nawab when he reached that town on his return journey from Calcutta, an act of clemency which has always been attributed to the influence of his grandmother, the old begum.

When, in the following year, Calcutta was recaptured by the English, and a temporary peace arranged between them and Suraj-ud-Dowlah, Mr. Watts returned to Murshedabad as Resident, and ran considerable risks from the nawab's ungovernable temper while negotiations were proceeding between him and Clive. In the end, Mr. Watts escaped secretly from Murshedabad, the nawab marched to meet Clive, and the Battle of Plassey swept away all the old order, and ushered in a new era. In 1760, Mr. Watts with his wife and children left India, and returned to England, where some years later he died. Mrs. Watts, who during her long residence in India had no doubt acquired many Eastern habits, and must have missed the luxury and authority of the old life, returned to India in 1769. Her daughters had both married, and her son was provided for, and in 1774 she once again entered the married state, and took for her fourth husband the Rev. William Johnson, the second, not the principal, presidency chaplain, as the epitaph states. The marriage does not appear to have been a success, for when he left India, some years later, his wife elected to remain behind, and lived on in Calcutta, "in a style of dignified hospitality," in her house "to the northward of the Old Fort," where she died on the 3rd of

February, 1812, at the great age of 87 years, It is not difficult to picture the old lady, in her hale old age, reclining among great cushions. waited on by attentive slave girls, enjoying the fragrant *hookah,* and telling over the oft-told tale of her experiences and adventures when under the protection of her friend the begum, whose title, so often on her lips, was turned by her friends in kindly jest into a *soubriquet* for herself. That the old lady was very particular about the observance of forms and ceremonies is shown by her having obtained from the Marquis of Wellesley the grant of a plot of ground, and permission that she might be buried in St. John's Churchyard, which had long been closed for interments, and also the promise that she should have a public funeral. When, in 1812, the time came for the fulfilment of these undertakings, Lord Wellesley had long vacated the Governor-Generalship, but his successor redeemed his pledge, and Begum Johnson was followed to her last resting-place by all the members of Calcutta society, headed by the Governor-General in his state coach, drawn by six horses, attended by the Body-Guard, and followed by the members of Council, and judges in their coaches.

CHAPTER VIII

TOLD BY THE TOMBS

Burying Ground Road (Park Street)—The Cemeteries–Tomb of Sir W. Jones, with contemporary account of his death and funeral—Col. Kyd, his will, details of his funeral, and site of his gave—Tombs connected with English literature: Richmond Thackeray, Col. Kirkpatrick, Rose Aylmer—Chambers' child, with some account of the loss of the *Grosvenor* East Indiaman.

WHEN Begum Johnson was laid to her last rest in St. John's Churchyard in 1812, that old burying-ground had been closed for interments for half a century. One of the earliest of the changes which, after Plassey, marked the transition of Calcutta from a fortified settlement to a town, was the formation of a new burial-place for the dead, away from the dwellings of the living, since there was no longer the need to keep it sheltered under the guns of the Fort. The proceedings of the Board for September 29, 1766, record—

"The present burying-ground, situate in the middle of the town, is very detrimental to the health of the inhabitants, and too much confined: the Civil Architect is therefore directed to point out a more convenient situation for one to be made of proper dimensions."

A year later, in August, 1767, the president acquainted the Board that the new burying-ground was ready; and on the same day, the 25th of August, the first funeral took place there: it was that of Mr. Wood, a writer in the Council House, whose grave was obliterated later, when the cemetery was enlarged by the addition of a piece of ground to the south. Mr. Wood's grave did not remain solitary for long. The recorded burials of the period average two hundred a year, and soon the heavy monuments arose and multiplied on every side, as the City of the Dead gathered in its denizens. A description of the Park Street cemeteries, as they appeared in 1785, is to be found in the letters of Sophia Goldborne, in "Hartly House, Calcutta:"—

"Alas! Arabella," wrote the young lady in saddened strain, "the Bengal burying-grounds (for there are two of them) bear a melancholy testimony to the truth of my observations on the short date of existence in this climate. . . . Obelisks, pagodas, etc., are erected at great expense; and the whole spot is surrounded by as well-turned a walk as those you traverse in

Kensington Gardens, ornamented with a double row of aromatic trees, which afford a solemn and beautiful shade: in a word, not old Windsor Churchyard, with all its cypress and yews, is in the smallest degree comparable to them; and I quitted them with unspeakable reluctance.

"There is no difference between these two grounds, but in the expense of the monuments which denote that persons of large fortune are there interred, and *vice versâ:* whence, in order to preserve this difference in the appearance, the first ranks pay five hundred rupees, the second three hundred, for opening the ground; and they are disjoined merely by a broad road."

It is not quite clear whether the two burying-grounds thus described are those now known as the North and South Park Street burying-grounds, which lie opposite to each other on either side of Park Street, or whether the description applied to the older, the South Ground only. The earliest epitaph in the North Ground, given in that quaint compilation, the "Bengal Obituary," is dated 1791, some six or seven years later than the period of the letters.

When the South Park Street Burying Ground was opened it was surrounded by fields, and was far in the country, though it is many years now

SIR W. JONES'S MONUMENT.

ROSE AYLMER'S MONUMENT.

[Face p. 153.

since the ever-widening boundaries of the town passed far beyond. A road was constructed along which funerals might pass to it through fields and by outlying hamlets. This road, known to Modern Calcutta as Park Street, was called Burying Ground Road, and many were the mournful processions which slowly trod its dreary length, as described by Miss Goldborne :—

"Funerals are indeed solemn and affecting things at Calcutta," she wrote, "no hearses being here introduced, or hired mourners employed; for as it often happens, in the gay circles, that a friend is dined with one day and the next is in eternity, the feelings are interested, the sensations awful, and the mental question, for the period of interment at least, which will be to-morrow's victim? The departed one, of whatever rank, is carried on men's shoulders (like your walking funerals in England), and a procession of gentlemen, equally numerous and respectable from the extent of genteel connections, following—the well-situated and the worthy being universally esteemed and caressed while living, and lamented when dead."

One of the most conspicuous monuments in the South Ground is that which marks the grave of Sir William Jones, and bears the following epitaph, remarkable no less for the noble sentiments expressed, than from the fact that it was written by himself:—

Here was deposited the mortal part of a man
Who feared God, but not death,
And maintained independence,
But sought not riches; who thought
None below him but the base and unjust,
None above him but the wise and virtuous;
Who loved
His parents, kindred, friends, and country,
With an ardour
Which was the chief source of
All his pleasures and all his pains:
And who, having devoted
His life to their service, and to
The improvement of his mind, resigned it calmly,
Giving Glory to his Creator,
Wishing peace on earth
And with good will to all creatures.
On the twenty-seventh day of April,
In the year of our blessed Redeemer,
One thousand seven hundred and ninety-four.

The lofty obelisk, its clear-cut lines towering far above the surrounding structures, is typical of him who sleeps below, whose name similarly dominates all others in the history of the decade during which he laboured in Bengal.

Sir William Jones arrived at Calcutta in 1783, to take up the office of a puisne judge of the Supreme Court, and the account of his reception given by his biographer indicates the high place which he at once took in public estimation, a place which he held with increasing honour to the last.

"His reputation," says the record, "had preceded his arrival, which was anxiously expected, and he had the happiness to find that his appointment had diffused a general satisfaction, which his presence now rendered complete. The students of the Oriental languages were eager to welcome a scholar, whose erudition in that branch of literature was unrivalled, and whose labours and genius had assisted their progress; while the public rejoiced in the possession of a magistrate whose probity and independence were no less acknowledged than his abilities."

One of Sir William Jones's earliest acts in India was the founding of the Asiatic Society, and, for ten years, he laboured with indefatigable zeal and stupendous learning, carrying out his duties on the Bench with care and dignity, studying Sanskrit, writing voluminously, translating learnedly, and attending the weekly meetings of the Society he had founded, and to which he contributed many valuable papers, notably his discourses as president. In one of these, the seventh, it is curious to note that, according to a writer in the *Calcutta Review* for September, 1846, he, after discussing the Chinese and their origin, as a people who are mentioned in *Manu* as a race of outcast Hindus, "noticed Japan, the Britain of the East, colonized by Hindus

1300 B.C., where Hindu idolatry prevailed from the earliest ages."

In the midst of these manifold labours, and in the prime of life—he was just forty-seven,—Sir William Jones was, in 1794, stricken with a mortal malady. His wife, whom he had married on his obtaining the Indian appointment, had been in poor health, and he had sent her to England, intending to follow her in a year's time, on the completion of a work on Hindu law on which he was engaged, so that he was living alone in his house at Garden Reach. Although the particulars of his pathetic and lonely death are well known, the following extracts from the diary of one of his Calcutta contemporaries have a melancholy interest, and give a vivid sense of the strength of the feelings of attachment and regard which the great scholar and remarkable man inspired.

"April 27th, 1794. Received the information that Sir William Jones was no more! I confess it struck me severely, and, in the bitterness of my grief, I almost cursed my own existence to think that such *really* great and good men as he should be thus snatched away, whilst the wicked and ignorant are permitted not only to walk this planet, but to commit their depredations upon it! Whatever is, is right!

"April 28th. Arose at five. W. and I rode on horseback to the west of the Fort, round by the eastward to Chowringhee, where we waited upwards of an hour to see the funeral of Sir William Jones pass by. All the European troops in garrison were there, with clubbed arms.

"April 30th. In conversation this day with R. about Sir William Jones, whose lamented death lies uppermost in my mind. He told me he had been ill for about a week or ten days (or rather complained of being ill about that period) before his death. Doctor Hare attended him, . . . and found on the right side a tumour as big as his fist. Inquiring when this came, he said it appeared about four or five months ago, but that, as it came of itself, he imagined it would go away in the same manner, and had taken no notice of it, only by way of exercise had walked every day before his carriage to and from the Garden, upwards of four miles. On being asked if it had not been very painful, he replied that it had been so very severe that he would not go through such another period for all the riches and honours in the world. On hearing this, one is tempted to call out, 'Oh! the *weakness* of a *strong* mind!' He said he thought it beneath him to let the mind bend to the pains of the body. He must have been delirious much longer than they think, as he would not let any one approach him, not even his favourite slave-boy Otho. R. said Sir

John Shore had even offered to sit up with him, but he answered he was better, and his mind quite easy.

"On Saturday night the doctors thought him better, and had recommended him to go home, either on the *Boddington* or *Sugar Cane*, Botany Bay ships, by which time they hoped to have him able to undertake the voyage, proposing first to salivate him. Early on Sunday morning the *consomah* ran over to Sir John Shore's, and said his master was *mad*, by which he understood he was delirious, and went there accompanied by Sir Robert Abercromby, the General. Just as they came to the premises another servant came out, and said that, since the *consomah* had left the house, Sir William had called for a dish of tea, drank it, and died! On their entrance they found him reclining on the couch, his head against his right hand, and the forefinger upwards towards the forehead, his usual attitude—his extremities were warm. Thus ended the mortal career of that truly great man Sir William Jones."

There is one sentence in the above extracts, penned as they were in a spirit of genuine admiration and manly grief, that strikes a jarring note to the modern ear. "His favourite slave-boy Otho," reads strangely, and it is hard to reconcile the master of the slave with the judge who, in one of his charges to the Calcutta Grand Jury,

SIR WILLIAM JONES.

LT.-COL. ROBERT KYD.

[*Face p.* 158.

condemned the practice of slavery in these forcible words :—

"Hardly a man or woman exists in a corner of this populous town who hath not at least one slave-child, either purchased at a trifling price, or saved perhaps from a death, that might have been fortunate, for a life that seldom fails of being miserable. Many of you, I presume, have seen large boats filled with such children, coming down the river for open sale at Calcutta: nor can you be ignorant that most of them were stolen from their parents, bought, perhaps, for a measure of rice in a time of scarcity, and that the sale itself is a defiance of this Government by violating one of its positive orders, which was made some years ago, after a consultation of the most reputable Hindus in Calcutta, who condemned such a traffic, as repugnant to their *Sástra*. The number of small houses in which these victims are pent, make it indeed very difficult for the settlement at large to be apprised of their condition: and if the sufferers knew where or how to complain, their very complaints may expose them to still harsher treatment: to be tortured if remanded, or, if set at liberty, to starve."

This picture of slavery in Calcutta at the close of the eighteenth century, horrible as it is, was by no means overdrawn, and the hideous custom did not die out till nearly fifty years after that period. There are old people still living who can tell of the time when slave boys and girls were ordinary inmates of numbers of European households in Calcutta—children, the larger number of whom had been bought for three or four rupees, from dealers who in turn had purchased them for "a measure of rice" from their starving parents in a famine year, or rescued them from flooded homesteads when the country was swept by a storm-wave, or perhaps snatched them by stealth from the river's bank, where hapless babes were left to perish by the side of a dying or dead mother, the victim of a ghastly "ghat murder" perpetrated in the name of religion.

That the custom of keeping slaves was a recognized one in spite of its being against the order of the Government, we find, not only from the mention of Sir William Jones's boy Otho, but also from another document of the same period, the will of Lieut.-Colonel Robert Kyd, who also lies in the South Park Street Burial Ground. By his will, dated 18th May, 1793, a week before his death, Colonel Kyd left legacies, of six rupees and eight rupees monthly respectively, to two boys, Missah and George, "as reparation for having been taken away from their home and friends, and the latter converted to Christianity by his former master, and taken from his own tribe, believed Rajpoots."

A very different type of man to Sir William Jones, Lieut.-Colonel Kyd stands out an interesting figure among old Calcutta worthies, and his name should be held in grateful remembrance as the founder of the beautiful Botanic Gardens. When Colonel Kyd, in 1786, first made his proposal to the East India Company to establish a Botanic Garden, he was Military Secretary to Government. Ten years earlier he had visited the then "eastern frontier," the western borders of Assam, and had brought from there young plants of a species of cinnamon which he had found growing wild there. Within the next few years other specimens had been obtained from Bhutan, and still other plants of the true cinnamon from Ceylon. All these plants were "deposited in the Governor-General's garden," the "well-stocked garden" of Warren Hastings' "old house" in Alipore; and there they throve so well, that it was on their successful transplantation to Bengal that Colonel Kyd laid stress, as proving the usefulness and practicability of his scheme. As Ceylon and the profitable cinnamon trade was at that time in the hands of the Dutch, the Board of Directors readily agreed to a proposal which seemed to promise a prospect of successful competition, the proposed garden was sanctioned, and Colonel Kyd was appointed honorary superintendent, a post which he held till his death, seven years later, in 1793.

Colonel Kyd had a house at Shalimar, in the neighbourhood of Howrah, on the opposite bank of the river to Calcutta, and adjoining the grounds was a plot of land which was selected for the Botanical Garden. The eastern end of this strip of land, which lay along the river-bank, was separated from Colonel Kyd's own grounds of Shalimar only by a ditch, crossed by a masonry bridge. All this portion of the garden—which had been occupied by a few native huts, whose owners, having no other title than possession, were compensated and removed—was laid out as a teak plantation, with the idea of obtaining timber for the Company's navy. But the trees did not thrive, and thirty-four years later, the experiment having proved a failure, the land was made over by the Government to Bishop Middleton, as a site for Bishop's College, founded in 1820. At the same time, a portion of Colonel Kyd's old garden was presented to the College by Sir C. T. Metcalfe, who then owned the property. The whole site is now in the occupation of the Engineering College, for which the

Government purchased it from the Society for the Propagation of the Gospel, when Bishop's College was removed to Calcutta, in 1879.

The lower, or western, end of the Botanical Garden was the land which had been occupied by the old native fort of Tanna or Muckwah Thanna, which stood just about the position of the superintendent's house, and was a Mohammedan outpost built to protect the trade of the river. At the end of the seventeenth century, when the Hughly River was infested with Portuguese pirates, the Mohammedan Governor of Bengal had a chain kept at Tanna Fort, which used to be fastened across the river to bar the passage of the buccaneers should they be tempted to sail up stream, to loot the villages of the wealthy traders of the higher reaches.

After the establishment of the Botanical Gardens, Colonel Kyd continued to reside in his house at Shalimar, which he had built, and to which he was much attached. It is pathetic to read, in his will, the careful dying directions for the up-keep of his garden and the care of his household till the return to India of his relative and heir, Major, afterwards General, Alexander Kyd, and his instructions regarding the disposal of his unfinished collections of botanical drawings of the plants in the environs, of birds indigenous to this tract, also of the fish frequenting the Hughly. "These," he wrote, "having been collected at the Company's expense, are public property, and should be transmitted to the Court of Directors, although unarranged in botanical or artificial order, which I had reserved for a future day."

Saddest of all are the sentences in which he directs that his "last remains be committed to the ground, in my own garden, on the west side of the Pucka Walled Tank, near to where an Alligator tree now stands, and that my funeral expenses do not exceed rupees three hundred."

These last directions were disregarded: it was probably felt that it would be improper to give so honoured and distinguished a servant of the Company so obscure a burial, and Colonel Kyd was buried, by order of Sir John Shore, in the South Park Street Burying Ground, at a cost of over eight hundred rupees. Although the funeral was conducted with much pomp and ceremony, including "hearse with velvet and plumes and best pall" and "two men in black with dressed staffe, etc., to precede the corpse," and was followed by fifty-three mourners in "black silk scarfs and hatbands," the grave itself, which was made just within the gate of the burying-ground, immediately to the right on entering, remained unmarked by tablet or monument. An oblong platform of masonry, it was for years utilized as the foundation for a hut used by the native gardeners; then it fell into ruins, and, finally, a well was sunk on the very spot, and every trace of the grave obliterated, and so at last the wish of the quiet lover of nature was gratified.

There are three graves in the Park Street cemeteries which are closely associated with English literature: they are those of the Honourable Miss Aylmer, of Richmond Thackeray, and of Lieut.-Colonel James Achilles Kirkpatrick. The two latter are in the North Burying Ground, but that of Miss Aylmer is in the South Ground, not far from that of Sir William Jones, and is marked by a graceful monument symbolical of the beautiful young life cut short—a fluted, tapering pillar, broken across, wreathed with drooping roses, joining inverted torches. It bears the following inscription:—

TO THE MEMORY OF THE HONOURABLE
ROSE WHITWORTH AYLMER
WHO DEPARTED THIS LIFE MARCH 2ND, A.D. 1800,
AGED 20 YEARS.

What was her fate? Long, long before her hour,
Death called her tender soul, by break of bliss,
From the first blossoms, to the buds of joy:
Those few our noxious fate unblasted leaves
In this inclement clime of human life.

Miss Aylmer went to Calcutta, to her aunt, Lady Russell, the wife of Sir Henry Russell, one of the judges of the Supreme Court; and it was in their house in Chowringhee, the house which gave its name to Russell Street, to which the grounds extended at the back, that she died. The event was announced in the *Calcutta Gazette* in the following terms:—

"On Sunday last, at the house of her uncle, Sir Henry Russell, in the bloom of youth, and possession of every accomplishment that could gladden and embellish life, deplored by her relatives and regretted by a society of which she was the brightest ornament, the Honourable Miss Aylmer."

Before Rose Aylmer left England for India, she had met Walter Savage Landor, and had inspired in him a romantic tenderness which breathes in the melodious lines he wrote on receiving the news of her death, and in which her name is enshrined in English poetry.

"Ah! what avails the sceptred race?
   Ah! what the form divine?
What every virtue, every grace?
   Rose Aylmer, all were thine.
Rose Aylmer, whom these wakeful eyes
   May weep but never see,
A night of memories and of sighs
   I consecrate to thee."

Another love romance was closed for ever

when James Kirkpatrick, the brilliant soldier-administrator of Hyderabad, was, in 1805, laid in his grave in the North Burying Ground, a grave which is lost among the crowding tombs, whose inscriptions have in many cases been rendered illegible by weather stains and the wear of time. According to the "Bengal Obituary," Kirkpatrick's tomb bore an inscription similar to that on a monument which was placed in St. John's Church, which reads as follows :—

To the memory of

LIEUT.-COLONEL JAMES ACHILLES KIRKPATRICK,

Of the Honourable East India Company's Military Establishment
of Fort St. George,
Who, after filling the distinguished station as Resident
at the Court of Hyderabad upwards of nine years,
And successfully conducting during that period various
important negociations,
Died at Calcutta, 15th October, 1805, aged 41 years,
This Monument is erected by his afflicted father and brothers.

Transcendent art! whose magic skill alone,
Can soften rock, and animate a stone,
By symbol mark the heart, reflect the head,
And raise a living image from the dead!
Cease from these toils, and lend the chisel's grace
To filial virtues courting your embrace.

These relate his pride, his transport, and relief;
A father's tears commemorate with grief!
Still while their genial lustre cheers his breast
Emits a ray that points to blissful rest:
Hope built on Faith, affection's balm and cure,
Divinely whispers, "Their reward is sure." (J. K.)

As Resident at the court of the Nizam of Hyderabad, Lieut.-Colonel Kirkpatrick rendered valuable services to the Government under the Marquis of Wellesley, and firmly established British authority in that State, at a time when the French were powerful rivals in Southern India; but it is his personal history that draws attention and arouses a lively interest even after the lapse of a hundred years.

In Hyderabad, Kirkpatrick was known by the Indian title *Husheerat Jung*, or "Glorious-in-battle." He was a great favourite with the nizam, who built a splendid palace for him as Residency, and there he lived, in all the magnificence and style of an Indian noble, with a beautiful young begum who had lost her heart to the handsome soldier, and threatened to take her own life if he persisted in the refusal of her suit.

When the young girl herself, "in faint and broken accents," pleaded her love, and was supported by her mother and grandmother, Kirkpatrick, as he wrote his brother, "must have been something more or less than man to have held out any longer," and the pair were married by civil contract according to the Mohammedan law. The alliance caused no little stir and scandal, and Lord Wellesley contemplated superseding the Resident. But Kirkpatrick's great public services, and the importance of his personal influence at a critical period, condoned his fault, and he and his princess remained undisturbed in their happiness till 1805. By that time their two children, a boy and a girl, were three and five years old respectively; Kirkpatrick decided to send them to England to his father, and to proceed himself to Calcutta, to confer with Lord Cornwallis, who had taken over the Government, and also for the benefit of his health, which had broken down.

The children were embarked at Madras, where they parted from their parents, who were never to meet again. Kirkpatrick sailed for Calcutta, where he died soon after his arrival: the poor young begum returned alone to her splendid home, desolate at once of husband and children, and died a few years later, and so closed in sadness and loneliness the passionate romance.

The children grew up happily in their English home; the son died in early manhood, leaving a widow and three children; the daughter, who also married, lived to a great age. She was in her youth the beautiful Kitty Kirkpatrick who made so deep an impression on Carlyle, and was the original of his "Blumine" in "Sartor Resartus." In his "Reminiscences," Carlyle recalled his first sight of her, when he had just arrived on a visit to Edward Irving and his wife :—

"Dash of a brave carriage driving up, and entry of a strangely complexioned young lady, with soft brown eyes, and floods of bronze-red hair, rather a pretty-looking, smiling, and amiable, though most foreign bit of magnificence and kindly splendour, whom they welcomed by the name of 'dear Kitty.' Kitty Kirkpatrick, Charles Buller's cousin or half cousin, Mrs. Strachey's full cousin, with whom she lived: her birth, as I afterwards found, an Indian romance. Mother a sublime begum, father a ditto English official, mutually adoring, wedding, living withdrawn in their own private Paradise, romance famous in the East. A very singular 'dear Kitty' who seemed bashful withal, and soon went away, twitching off in the lobby, as I could notice, not without wonder, the loose label which was sticking to my trunk or bag, still there as she past, and carrying it off in her pretty hand."

Again Carlyle wrote :—

"Mrs. Strachey, Mrs. Buller's younger sister, took to me from the first nor ever swerved. It strikes me now more than it then did, she silently could have liked to see 'dear Kitty' and myself come together, and so continue near her, both of us, through life. The good, kind soul! And

Kitty, too, was charming in her beautiful Begum sort, had wealth abundant, and might perhaps have been charmed, none knows. She had one of the prettiest smiles, a visible sense of humour, the slight merry curl of the upper lip (right side of it only), the carriage of her head and eyes on such occasions, the quaint little things she said in that kind, and her low-toned hearty laugh were noticeable. This was perhaps her most spiritual quality; of developed intellect she had not much, though not wanting in discernment: amiable, affectionate, graceful, might be called attractive, not slim enough for the title pretty, not tall enough for beautiful, had something low-voiced, languidly harmonious, loved perfumes, etc., a half-Begum in short, an interesting specimen of the semi-oriental English woman."

A subtle, fascinating picture this, which forms a delicate glittering link between the rugged figure of grim Thomas Carlyle, and the brilliant soldier who lorded it so proudly among the nobles of Hyderabad, and rests so quietly in his time-worn tomb, in the North Park Street Burying Ground.

Close to where Kirkpatrick lies in his soldier-grave, is the square brick-built monument which marks the grave of the civilian Richmond Thackeray, the father of William Makepeace Thackeray. Richmond was the son of an earlier

William Makepeace Thackeray who, as Sir W. W. Hunter has told, made a very large fortune during his eleven years' service in Bengal as Resident at Sylhet, chiefly by the capture of wild elephants, which he sold to his honourable masters, at a handsome profit to himself. Sylhet Thackeray married, in Calcutta, in 1776, a daughter of Lieut.-Colonel Richmond Webb, and retired from India the year after, at the age of twenty-eight, to live in comfort and style for thirty-five years in England, from where he sent out to India six sons and three daughters, out of his family of twelve children.

Of the sons, two spent some years in Calcutta, and died there: Richmond, the civilian, and Charles, a barrister. Clever, witty, an able writer, and a charming companion, Charles Thackeray fell a victim to his own convivial tastes. His practice at the Bar was of the slightest, but he was on the staff of the leading Calcutta newspaper, the then newly created *Englishman*, and might have prospered but for the vice which dragged him down. He lived for many years in Alipore, at No. 12, and died in the early forties of the last century, leaving none to mourn him, or to place a kindly record on his grave. His brother died some thirty years before him, in September, 1815. Richmond Thackeray arrived

RICHMOND THACKERAY'S TOMB.

KIERNANDER FAMILY VAULT.

[Face p. 173.

in India in 1798, at the age of sixteen, and filled various district appointments, till, in 1807, he became secretary to the Board of Revenue in Calcutta. Here he married Miss Becher, daughter of another old civilian family, and here, on the 18th of July, 1811, was born his famous son: if tradition be true, in the house which became later the Armenian convent. Before his little son was six months old, Richmond Thackeray became Collector of the Twenty-four Pergunnahs, and removed with his family to Alipore, where they lived in the house which had been "The Lodge" of Philip Francis. There he died, four years later, and from there the long procession of his funeral made its way down the oft-trodden road to the Park Street Burial Ground. His long and formal epitaph thus records his virtues, and the admiration of his friends:—

To the Memory of
RICHMOND THACKERAY, ESQRE.,
late on the Bengal Establishment of the
Honourable East India Company,
who expired on the 13th September, 1815,
at the premature age of 32 years,
10 months, and 23 days.
To the best endowments of the understanding,
and to the purest principles in public life,
he united all the social and tender affections: under
the influence of these moral and intellectual
qualities he ever maintained the character of a
public officer with the highest degree of
credit to himself, and discharged in a manner

not less exemplary the duties which devolved upon
him in the several relations of private life.
To transmit to prosperity a memorial of
these virtues the present monument has been
erected by those who had the best means
of contemplating the habitual exercise of them
in the varied character of a son, a brother,
a husband, a father, and a friend.

Richmond Thackeray's tomb stands beside the western boundary wall of the cemetery; near it, crushed in by other dark and dismal monuments against the wall that separates the Mission Ground, is another tomb which deserves notice. It is that of William Jones, who in the early days of the nineteenth century was known in Calcutta as *Guru* Jones, the teacher, the master. As the discoverer of coal in India, Jones has a strong claim to be gratefully remembered. As an engineer and architect he did good service, and it was his professional skill, joined to his clear judgment and sterling worth, that won him the reverend title of *Guru* among his friends.

A shadowy mystery clings to the memory of *Guru* Jones, and suggests that he was the lost heir to an Irish dukedom. The story goes that, the youngest son of the late duke, he left his home through family quarrels, and sought his fortune in India, then the Land of Promise to every young adventurer. By the deaths of his father and brother the wanderer became the heir, but if he knew of the change in his fortunes he made no claim, and, failing his return, the title lapsed. Vague hints there are of letters that entreated the truant to return, of legal inquiries that strove to identify the lost heir, but whatever may have been the truth it lies buried under the grimy monument which records his widow's sense of his worth, and her regret, which no "pencil can describe, for the husband, the father, and the friend."

Jones was the architect of Bishop's College, Sibpur, and his death, which occurred on the 23rd of September, 1821, at the age of forty-four, was caused by a stroke of the sun while superintending the building. Bishop Middleton, the founder of the college, who himself died in the following year from the same cause, preached a funeral sermon on the death of William Jones, in which he spoke of the beautiful college as a noble monument to the memory of its architect.

Hard by the tomb of *Guru* Jones is a little wicket gate into the Mission Burial Ground, the plot of land which the Reverend J. Z. Kiernander bought in 1773, when he buried his wife there, and which later became the property of the trustees of the Mission Church. Here stands the heavy brick structure which Kiernander, as the inscription states, "caused to be erected as a testimony of sincere and affectionate regard" to the memory of his wife, and which marks the vault wherein he and many of his descendants are laid.

A short distance to the westward of the Mission Ground lies the fourth, and last, of the Park Street cemeteries, that known as the French or Tiretta's Burial Ground. This ground, like the Mission Ground, was purchased by a bereaved husband that he might there make a grave for his wife, and was subsequently presented by him to the members of his communion and their descendants. Edward Tiretta was an Italian of good family, who, having had to fly his own country for a political offence, drifted to Calcutta, where for many years he held the post of civil architect to Government, returning at last to his native land, where he died at an advanced age.

In 1796 Tiretta had the misfortune to lose his young wife, the orphan daughter of a French officer, the Count de Carrion, and he buried her in the Roman Catholic cemetery at Boitakhana, near Sealdah. Finding, however, that the graves in this cemetery were used repeatedly for fresh interments, he bought a plot of land near the other burial-grounds, and removed his wife's remains there, building over her grave a graceful monument with a Latin inscription. The new burial-ground thus established was presented by Tiretta to the Roman Catholic community, and the year after his wife's death a second grave was made there, that of his friend Mr. Mark Mutty, a Venetian, who, as the plain white marble slab which marks his grave records, died on the 2nd of August, 1797, aged thirty-seven years.

To chronicle all the tales of pathos and romance that whisper from the old tombs to the listening ear, would fill many volumes; but there is one sad story of the sea, that is connected with a grave in the South Ground, that should not be missed. Facing the heavy old gateway stands the "Family Tomb" of the Chambers, in which were laid, in February, 1782, the remains of Mrs. Anne Chambers, the mother of Sir Robert Chambers, afterwards Chief Justice of Bengal. The poor lady died of grief on parting with her grandchild, Sir Robert's eldest son. Mrs. Fay, who was at the time staying with Lady Chambers, recorded the sad event in her "Letters:"—

"Our friends left us on the 2nd instant," she wrote, "Sir R. and Lady C. felt severely the shock of their son's departure, but poor Mrs. C., whose very soul seemed treasured up, if I may so express myself, in her grandson, sank under the blow. On the 5th she was seized with a violent illness, of which, on the 7th, she expired. Sir R. is deeply affected, and I would be surprised if he were not, for to him she was ever an exemplary parent, and gave an irrefragable proof of strong maternal affection by accompanying him to this country at her advanced period of life. Her death is generally lamented as a most charitable, humane, good woman. 'Let her works praise her.' She was in her seventieth year. We came up here (Chinsurah) immediately after the funeral, which took place the next day, and was most numerously attended, I may say by almost the whole settlement, gentlemen as well as ladies. Her character demanded this testimony of respect, and that it was paid affords me pleasure."

Poor, tender soul! she was spared the bitter knowledge of the cruel fate which awaited the object of her affections. Within a year the bereaved parents placed upon her tomb a tablet which, fallen out now and cast away, bore this simple record of a great tragedy:—

To the Memory of
THOMAS FITZMAURICE CHAMBERS,
Son of Sir Robert and Lady Chambers,
Born on the 28th October, MDCCLXXVI.
Who was shipwrecked in the *Grosvenor*, and
Perished on the Coast of Africa, in August, 1782.

The *Grosvenor* East Indiaman sailed from the Hughly on her last ill-fated voyage on the

13th of January, 1782, and proceeded to Madras, where she lay for some weeks, taking in cargo. Among her intending passengers were a Mr. and Mrs. Hosea, with their young daughter. They came to Calcutta with the intention of sailing in her from that port, but Mrs. Hosea's health obliged them to allow the ship to sail without them, and to arrange to join her at Madras by a native vessel leaving Calcutta three weeks later. Their passage-money amounted to no less a sum than twenty thousand rupees, half of which amount would have been forfeited had they failed to meet the *Grosvenor* in time.

The Hoseas left Calcutta, as Mrs. Fay recorded, on the 2nd of February, taking with them the Chambers' six-year-old boy, and leaving in Lady Chambers' care a little infant twenty-five days old. In due course the *Grosvenor* sailed from Madras; five months later she had arrived off the east coast of Africa, and there, on the 3rd of August, 1782, she was cast away, at a point near Durban, on the shore of what was then an unexplored country, inhabited by savages, and five hundred miles from the nearest civilized settlement, a town of the Dutch, who then held the Cape.

The survivors of the wreck numbered no fewer than one hundred and thirty-five persons,

Europeans and natives. The officers and passengers mentioned in the accounts given in the papers of the time were the commander, Captain Coxon, and his three officers, Messrs. Logie, Shaw, and Beall; the purser, Mr. Hay; the chief mate's wife, Mrs. Logie; and passengers, Colonel and Mrs. James, Mr. and Mrs. Hosea with their daughter; two other girls, Miss Denis and Miss Wilmot; little Thomas Chambers, and another child, and Captain Adair, Mr. Nixon, and Mr. Newman, besides two native women, servants to Mrs. Hosea and Mrs. Logie.

Cast among savages who grew ever bolder and more threatening,—hampered by the sick, the injured, and the weakly,—cut off from every prospect of escape by sea, the unfortunate castaways essayed the impossible task of marching through an unknown and hostile country, in the hope of reaching the Dutch settlement five hundred miles away. Starting in a body, they soon broke up into parties, the strongest hurrying forward trusting to be able to reach their goal and bring back help to their weaker companions. Gradually the numbers dwindled, disease, privation, and exposure destroyed those who escaped the hands of the savages, and, in the end, of all that crowded ship's company eighteen alone survived to return to their friends. Of these, six men succeeded in reaching the Dutch settlement after a perilous journey of one hundred and seventeen days ; and three sailors, seven lascars, and the two women servants were rescued, nearly two years later, by the first of several expeditions which were sent out at different times by the Dutch to search for any of the survivors.

With the rescue of these eighteen persons, the story of the wreck of the *Grosvenor* closed in contemporary records, but, as years passed on, again and yet again came strange rumours of English women being seen in Kaffir *kraals*, dressed in Kaffir fashion, and refusing to leave their savage surroundings, on the plea that they had become contented mothers of families, and were no longer willing or able to return to their old lives. During the Kaffir war of 1835, a curious incident partly raised the veil of doubt and mystery which enwrapped the fate of the lost lady-passengers. A tribe of native warriors offered their services as "brothers" to the English against their own countrymen, the Kaffirs, saying that their tribe, which numbered six hundred souls, were descendants of the English ladies who had been wrecked in the *Grosvenor* fifty-three years before, and now, at this day, that tribe stands out distinct from its fellows. And when men visit the rugged coast of Zululand,

and, looking down through the clear waters, see the weed-grown guns and iron that mark the spot where lay the wreck, they tell again the story of the lost East Indiaman, and their thoughts rest in pity on the shadowy pathetic figures of those English women who, dead to their former world and all that they held most dear, lived out their lives as wives and mothers among an alien and savage race.

A STREET SCENE IN THE NATIVE QUARTER, 1792.

[Face p. 183.

CHAPTER IX

STREETS AND HOUSES

Old maps—Names of streets—Docks—The main drain—The Creek—Government House Grounds—The Militia and their Parade Ground—Street scenes—Executions—Old houses—Sudder Street, Park Street—Boitakhana tree.

IN studying the history of Calcutta it is the personal element that lays the strongest hold on the imagination; the glimpses that are caught of lives full of incident, and often of romance, are so suggestive, that they make one long to pierce the dark shadows that time has cast over all but the few prominent figures who rise high enough above their fellows to catch the light thrown backwards by history. In some few cases it is possible to piece together a chapter in a life, of the earlier portion of which no record remains, but of which the *finis* was written on a Calcutta tombstone which has long since crumbled to dust.

One such fragment of a life-story tells of Aaron Upjohn, who, though one of the humblest of Calcutta citizens in his day, perpetuated his name by a map of Calcutta, which he published in 1794, and for which every student of the past history of the town must be grateful.

Upjohn's life was one of adventure, and he experienced many changes of fortune. He reached India in the humble capacity of bassoon player in the band of Captain Wakeman, commander of the *Rodney*, a position to which we may conclude he had been driven by circumstances, for his varied attainments prove him to have been a man of some education. Possibly the desire to escape importunate creditors suggested the comparatively easy method of obtaining a passage to a land beyond their reach.

Upjohn next appears as a printer, and holder of a one-sixth share in the *Chronicle*. This journal, which had its offices in Bow Bazaar, where the Police Office now stands, failed in 1797, but long before that date Upjohn had become bankrupt, and his share was sold by the mortgagee in 1792. In the same year, Upjohn began his survey for the map, which he completed and published in eighteen months, a feat which, so far from obtaining praise, was censured by his contemporary critics as proof of careless haste, as they considered that such an undertaking required at least two and a half years for its proper completion. The map was published at sixty rupees a copy, but poor Upjohn does not appear to have prospered as a surveyor. There is a fleeting glimpse of him trying to cultivate cochineal in an Alipore garden, and then, bankrupt once more, he passes finally off the stage, nor is his name to be found in that sad directory of the dead, the "Bengal Obituary."

An earlier map-maker than Upjohn was Captain, afterwards Lieut.-Colonel, Mark Wood, who in 1784–5 undertook a survey of the town for the commissioners of police. The work occupied over two years, and cost twenty-eight thousand rupees. This map showed each house in the town, and was on a scale of twenty-six and a half inches to the mile.

A reduced copy of Wood's map was issued in 1792 by Baillie, at the comparatively moderate price of twenty-five sicca rupees a copy, mounted on a roller, or twenty rupees if pasted on cloth. In his advertisement of this "Plan of Calcutta" in the *Calcutta Gazette*, Mr. Baillie excuses himself for a delay which had occurred in the publication, on the ground that he had been "waiting many months in the expectation that the streets in the native part of the town would have received new names, as those in the European quarter have lately done."

Some of the streets named at this time were, Old Court House Street, Old Post Office Street, and Old Fort Street, which included the present Dalhousie Square West, and Clive Street from Dalhousie Square to New China Bazar Street. Bankshall Street was also named about this time from the Marine House, known by the Dutch name of Bankshall, which, with the Master Attendant's Office, stood on the site now occupied by the Small Cause Court. This was the same house which, some thirty-five years earlier, had been the president's house outside the Fort. Another Dutch name then in use was Tackshall for the Custom House; this stood in the south-west angle of the Old Fort; and the street which led to it from the Great Tank was called Tackshall Street, now Koila Ghat Street. In Upjohn's map the name is printed "Tankshall Street," presumably a printer's error.

In 1790 the Company built a dock at the Bankshall, for their pilot vessels. The project was an old one, for, as far back as 1767, there being then no docks in Calcutta, a plan had been considered for building one between the Marine House and the Old Fort, and utilizing the whole space between these two points, for the erection of storehouses and other buildings. The proposal fell through, and by the time the "New Dock" was built, in 1790, to the west of the Marine House, several large docks had been built, not only on the Calcutta side of the river, but also on the opposite bank at Howrah and Sulkea. "The "New Dock" never became old, for, in 1808, it was filled up again, having apparently been of little use during the eighteen years it was open.

The earliest, as well as the most important, of the Calcutta docks was established about the year 1780, by Colonel Henry Watson, chief engineer under Warren Hastings' Government,—the Colonel Watson who acted as Francis's second in his duel with Hastings. Colonel Watson obtained from Government the grant of land at Kidderpore, "for the establishment of wet and dry docks and of a marine yard, in which every facility should be created for building, repairing, and equipping vessels of war, and merchantmen."

A feature of this dock, in Colonel Watson's scheme, was the utilization of the Govindpore Creek, which then joined the river some hundred yards further south than at present. He meant to use it as a backwater to scour out the Dock and Circular Basin, but Major Tolly, in his operations for rendering the Creek navigable, turned it further north, so that it passed round, instead of through, Colonel Watson's wet dock. Whether owing to this change, or from some other cause, Colonel Watson was unable to continue the work for more than a few years. He spent ten lakhs of rupees in the undertaking, and built, among other vessels, the *Nonsuch* frigate of thirty-six guns, launched in 1781, and the *Surprise* of thirty-two guns in 1788, soon after which date he withdrew from the enterprise. The Dock was then acquired by Mr. A. Waddell, the Company's master builder, who, on his retirement in 1807, was succeeded at the Docks, and in his post of master builder, by Mr. James Kyd, who had been his assistant for some years.

James Kyd, and his brother Robert, who became his partner, were sons of General Alexander Kyd; they were men of high character, and were widely respected, and greatly beloved for their generous charity. James survived his brother ten years, and on his death, in 1836, the Dock, in which many fine ships had been built, was acquired by the Government, and became the Government Dockyard, the sole survivor of the large number of dockyards which had once raised expectations that shipbuilding would become the leading industry of Calcutta.

One of the dockyards from which several good ships were launched was Gillet's Dockyard, which lay to the south of the New Dock at the Bankshall, opposite to the western entrance of St. John's Church. Some years later, when Gillet's Dock had been filled up, the site was occupied by the Calcutta Mint; and when this was removed, in 1829, to the New Mint, which had been built on the Strand, the Old Mint passed into the hands of Messrs. Moran & Co., indigo brokers. Long years afterwards, when this firm removed to Mango Lane, they carried with them the well-known designation of "The Old Mint Mart," to become a puzzle to later students of local topography.

In 1890, just one hundred years after the New Dock had been built, a portion of its walls were once more uncovered to the light of day, before being finally destroyed. In that year, the western extension of the Small Cause Court was built, and, in digging the foundations, the workmen disclosed masonry remains, which were easily identified as those of the New Dock, which, it was found, had measured fifty-three feet ten inches across, at the level of the first step.

The excavations of 1890, which uncovered

the remains of the New Dock, disclosed also a portion of a large drain in perfect order, which was readily recognized as the "main drain," by which the old open sewers of the town used to be flushed. This drain, which was found to lie about sixty feet back from the present roadway of Hare Street, was arranged to admit water from the river at high tides, by means of a sluice-gate. It ran underground from the river to Dalhousie Square, where it emerged, and continued its course as a surface drain. When, at suitable tides, the sluice was opened, the inrush of water, sweeping along this channel, flushed the principal sewers of the town, and finally found an outlet in the Creek, the remains of the old Calcutta creek, which had gradually been filled up as roads were made and houses built. The course of the Creek from the river had been eastward, along Hastings Street and Government Place, till it crossed Bentinck Street; here it took a sweep to the south, and so again eastward along the southern side of Dhurrumtolla Street, a locality marked in the old maps as Dinga Banga ("Broken or Wrecked Boat"), till it returned to a more northerly course near Wellington Square. From this point, till it found its way to the salt-water lakes at Belliaghatta, the old bed of the Creek remained, long after the closing of its connection with the river had deprived it of its stream, and turned it into a ditch which served to carry off the surface drainage. It was into this ditch, at what is now Wellington Square, that the sewers discharged their contents.

One of the improvements made in the town, at the beginning of the eighteenth century, was the filling up of as much of the Creek as remained between Circular Road and Wellington Square, which was then made, and laying a road along its course, which still bears the name it then received of Creek Row. About the same time, in 1805, the main drain was utilized for raising the level of the water in the Great Tank, Lal Diggie, by means of an open trench, connecting with the main drain exactly where the Dalhousie Institute now stands. In hot seasons, when the springs which supplied the tank failed to keep pace with the immense drain on them as the only source of a pure water-supply in the town, the river water used to be admitted through the main drain, and the tank kept at a proper level. That this process must have contaminated the tank water may well be imagined, when it is remembered that the river was polluted by the carcases of animals and human corpses, besides every possible form of pollution, so that its waters teemed with the germs of disease and death.

The Great Tank, it has been suggested, is fed by percolation from the river. It is of great depth, and there is a record, that when, in 1783–4, the tank was deepened, "at a depth of forty feet from the surface they found a regular row of trees, which, by the colour, seemed to be soondrie; they were pretty fresh. They were cut to the level of the bottom of the tank." There is a similar record respecting the tank which was made about 1794, and has been recently filled up, at the junction of Chowringhee Road and the Esplanade; and when the present Fort William was built, many traces of trees were found at a considerable depth below the surface of the ground. These remains are thought to be those of the great soondrie forest which once covered the site of Calcutta, when the land had newly emerged from the waters of the Gangetic Delta, which, shifting eastward, have left the once impassable tract to man, and have wrested from him what was a fertile and populated country, now a tangle of waterways among forest-hidden islands, which form the Soonderbunds.

It is something of a coincidence that as the opening years of the twentieth century have brought sweeping changes to Calcutta, and have seen the passing away of many old landmarks, and the creation of a new and more stately city, so the early years of the nineteenth century saw a similar changing of the old order ; and a similar desire for the improvement of the city as that which animates her citizens to-day, filled the minds of the men of Old Calcutta.

A hundred years ago a lottery was the most popular means of obtaining money for any purpose. For the building fund of St. John's Church ; in aid of the Free School ; for the sale of an indigo factory or a diamond ring, a lottery would be arranged. A date would be fixed for the drawing, a committee of independent gentlemen would give their services to see that it was properly carried out, and there were always purchasers ready to take their chances, at prices ranging from one gold mohur (sixteen rupees) to several hundred rupees a ticket, according to the value of the prizes offered. These were usually very valuable, a first prize of one lakh of rupees, in cash, being not unusual. Such a lottery was organized, in 1804, by "the inhabitants of Calcutta" for the erection of the Town Hall, in commemoration of the Administrations of Lord Cornwallis and Lord Wellesley. This lottery was on a grand scale, and was repeated in successive years ; so popular did it become that, in 1809, it was merged into a larger scheme of lotteries which were established "for the improvement of the town of Calcutta and its vicinity." These, the "Calcutta lotteries," were established by an order of the Governor-General in Council, to be "conducted by a superintendent, aided by a registrar and examiner, under the immediate control of commissioners appointed by Government;" and excellent work was carried out with the funds realized by them.

It is difficult now to distinguish between improvements carried out by the Lottery Committee, and changes effected at an earlier date, but from this period date some of the most important streets of the business quarter of the town, notably the Strand Road, from Chandpal Ghaut to the Mint, Hare Street, and Government Place North.

It should always be borne in mind, that the river's bank of the present day extends from fifty to two hundred and fifty yards further out than it did a century ago, when the waters flowed all along where are now busy wharves, and warehouses, and numerous buildings. At the northern end of the town, the Mayo Hospital stands on reclaimed ground; so does the Mint, which lies just beyond the highest spot of ground in Calcutta, the point where Cotton Street meets

Clive Street. Coming further south, the Small Cause Court is partly, and the Sailor's Home entirely, on ground recovered from the Hughly, so is the stately Metcalfe Hall. The Bank of Bengal stands where, in days before the English occupation, the native boatmen careened their craft, on the bank of the old Creek, at Cutchagoody Ghaut. In later years an avenue of trees marked this spot along the river-bank, and shaded the road known, from its neighbourhood to the Supreme Court, as King's Bench Walk. Another and a finer avenue of trees was planted, about the time of the Lottery Committee, on the river-bank from Chandpal Ghaut to the New Fort. This was known as Respondentia Walk, where Calcutta society, alighting from carriages and palanquins, promenaded in the cool of the evening; nor were dogs allowed to disturb the harmony of polite conversation, for an order of the Governor-General in Council forbade persons accompanied by dogs to be allowed in Respondentia Walk. Most of the old walk is included in the Eden Gardens, which were laid out under the direction of the Honble. Miss Eden and her sister, at the time their brother, Lord Auckland, was Governor-General, from 1836 to 1842.

It is not a little interesting and curious to

compare a view of this part of the river-bank, as it is at the present day, with Baillie's "General View of Calcutta," in 1794, which shows the same locality. When Baillie made his sketch, the trees of Respondentia Walk had not been planted, to intercept the view, and to-day only one or two gnarled old survivors of their once regular rows are left to mark where stretched the Promenade. The principal object in the modern view is the massive turreted building of the High Court. In Baillie's "View" the same site is occupied by the old Supreme Court, low, and dark in spite of its long verandah, which, with the two adjoining houses, made way for the present Court, so recently as in 1872.

The present-day picture shows, facing the Strand, the Bank of Bengal. When Baillie painted his "View" the King's Bench Walk crossed this spot, just above the muddy bank of the river, on which floated the wooden ships which the brave seamen of old sailed up the treacherous Hughly, under the guidance of the skilful pilots of the Ganges, and without the aid of steam or the service of tugs. Not more marked is the difference between these two pictures, of Calcutta at the end of the eighteenth century and Calcutta at the beginning of the

THE STRAND, CALCUTTA, 1900.

[Face p. 196.

twentieth century, than was the difference between the town, when it arose from its ruins after the siege, to what it became when, fifty years later, it was practically rebuilt.

The building, in the opening years of the eighteenth century, of a new Government House, which occupied the space where two of the largest of the old buildings had stood, and which dwarfed all others by comparison with its lofty proportions, not only gave a stimulus to the desire to improve the town, but obliged a re-arrangement of the streets in its immediate vicinity. The new Government House covered the entire space which had been sufficient for the old Government House, the Council House, and the grounds of both houses to the north. The two southerly wings of the new building rested on the Esplanade Road, while the two wings on the north extended to Wheler Place, a road which had formed the old boundary, and took its name from Mr. Wheler, member of Warren Hastings' Council, who, in 1784, in the Governor's absence, laid the foundation-stone of St. John's Church. This road led from old Court House Street to a large private house, probably "Mr. Wheler's house," which stood just where the north-west wing of Government House ends. The house was pulled down, as were five other dwelling-houses; Wheler Place, carried through to Council House Street, became, as it remains to this day, the carriage-drive within the gates, and the Government House grounds were extended to the north to a new road, Government Place, which was made in continuation of Hastings Street, and from which another new road, Wellesley Place, was made to lead to Tank Square. Fancy Lane, Larkin's Lane, and Vansittart Row still remain what they were, but Corkscrew Lane, which led by devious twists from Wheler Place to Fancy Lane, was improved away.

Another new road made in this neighbourhood was Hare Street, which replaced one of two narrow lanes, which led to the river from an open space lying between the Bankshall and St. John's Churchyard. A strip from the churchyard was taken to widen Church Lane, and the new road was laid to form a continuation of the Tank Square Road to the river-bank, which was considerably advanced. It was named after Mr. David Hare, the philanthropic watchmaker, the pioneer of native education in Calcutta, who lived in a house opposite to Bankshall Street, the wide grounds of which adjoined the churchyard.

On the north side of Dalhousie Square stands one of the oldest public buildings existing in

Calcutta, the handsome range of offices now known as the Bengal Secretariat, but which for nearly a century bore the name of Writers' Buildings.

The late Mr. Reginald Craufuird Sterndale, while Collector of Calcutta in 1884, found among the records of that office the original *pottah* of the land which was granted in October, 1776, to Mr. Thomas Lyon, "for the purpose of erecting a range of buildings for the accommodation of the junior servants of the company." Although the land was granted to Mr. Lyon, whose name has been perpetuated in Lyon's Range, the street behind the "Range," Mr. Sterndale was of opinion that he acted in the matter on behalf of Mr. Richard Barwell, the friend and steady supporter in council of Warren Hastings. Whether this was the case, or Barwell purchased the property from Lyon, he was the acknowledged owner in 1780, the year in which the building was completed and was taken by the Government on a five years' lease, when Francis wrote in his journal, "Mr. Barwell's house taken for five years by his own vote. Mr. Wheler and I declare we shall not sign the lease."

The Buildings contained nineteen sets of apartments, each furnished with a separate set of out-offices, and the rent was two hundred Arcot rupees per month for each set of apartments—a handsome income for their owner.

Previous to the erection of Writers' Buildings, private houses had been leased by Government as required for the occupation of the young writers, who received free quarters, and, in common with all civil servants, drew numerous allowances in the way of diet money, palanquin hire, and, in the case of the seniors, family allowances and house-rent. In 1785, new rules were issued as to the pay and allowances of the Company's civil servants, and it was then ordered that all writers drawing less pay than three hundred rupees per month should be allowed quarters in the "New Buildings," two to each house, or set of apartments, and should receive one hundred rupees a month in lieu of all former allowances, the right to quarters to cease on being appointed to an office the salary of which exceeded three hundred rupees a month.

For nearly fifty years Writers' Buildings continued in the use for which it was originally intended, and maintained a reputation for fast living and extravagance of every kind, which was only natural under the circumstances. The youthful writer, arriving in India, released from the irksome monotony of a weary six months' voyage, and free for the first time from the strict

WRITERS' BUILDINGS AND THE HOLWELL MONUMENT, 1792.

[*Face p.* 200.

control of his pastors and masters, was prepared to bear his part bravely in the reckless expenditure and wild excesses which he found to be the fashion among his fellow-writers. Lord Valentia, writing in 1803, of the young writers' training in Calcutta, said—

"There are few of these young men who do not keep their horses, commonly their curricles, and, in many instances, their race-horses, which, together with the extravagant parties and entertainments frequent among them, generally involve them in difficulties and embarrassments at an early period of their lives."

The costly champagne suppers of Writers' Buildings were famous, and long did the old walls echo to "the joyous songs and loud rehearsing tally-hoes" of many generations of writers. Gradually, however, there came a change; the age for entering the Company's civil service was raised, the period of a writer's stay in Calcutta was reduced, and, at last, writers were no longer provided with quarters, but lived with friends, or in lodgings at their own expense. For some years Writers' Buildings remained deserted; then the sets of apartments were let to private individuals and for offices. The next change saw them occupied as Government offices;

and, lastly, came alterations and additions which crowned the old bare range with domes, and masked it with a stately façade, and Writers' Buildings were lost in the Bengal Secretariat.

Before leaving this, the oldest quarter of the town, it is well to recall that, up to about 1810, the southern portion of Dalhousie Square, a strip of land about two hundred and fifty yards long by fifty yards wide, at the south-west end of which stood the stables of the Governor's Body-guard, was the Parade Ground, on which the Militia and Volunteers of Calcutta paraded.

It was in 1752 that the Worshipful Court of Directors sent orders to Calcutta that a body of Militia should be formed; and, in September of that year, the Calcutta Board reported that—

> "in obedience to your Honour's orders, Captain Commandant George Minchin proposes, as soon as the weather sets in a little more temperate, to fix and appoint proper sergeants and corporals, out of the military, for instructing such of the inhabitants as are unacquainted with the manual exercise, when we shall appoint officers to command them."

In November, accordingly, the new officers of the Militia, Colonel Cruttenden in command, were ordered to "attend on the Parade on Monday, 20th November, at six of the clock, in the morning." A week later, it was notified that, "several of the inhabitants of this town having absented themselves from attending the Militia," a list of their names was to be affixed at the Fort gates, and, in case of future non-attendance, "they may expect to meet with proper resentment from the Board." Evidently the new orders were unpopular, and the threat too vague to induce obedience, for four years later, in 1756, the Court in severe terms desired to know the reason why a Militia had not been formed, and insisted that their orders should be carried out without delay, "as, at this time in particular, a regular Militia may be of the greatest importance for the defence of the settlement."

This grave warning must have risen accusingly in the minds of many members of the Calcutta Board, when, a few weeks later, they hurriedly prepared to defend Calcutta against the army of Suraj-ud-Dowlah. On the approach of the nawab, a body of Militia two hundred and fifty strong, including Europeans, Armenians, and Portuguese, was hurriedly got together, under the command of civilian officers, among them Mr. Holwell, commanding the first company, and the junior chaplain, the Reverend Robert Mapletoft, as one of the captain-lieutenants. Several others of the Company's civil servants formed themselves into a company of Volunteers, and did excellent service. The Militia, too, fought well in the earlier part of the siege, but became disheartened, and finally collapsed in abject fear, adding greatly to the difficulties of the defenders.

After the fall of Calcutta, the Militia were re-organized at Fulta, and we can fancy that drilling at that time was carried out in deadly earnest. Many of the Company's servants joined the Regulars, but the others formed a company of Volunteers, who marched, and fought with Clive's troops at the recapture of Calcutta and in the operations that followed. Colonel Broome, in his "History of the Bengal Army," states that when, in October, 1759,—

"a Dutch fleet arrived in the river, with seven hundred Europeans and eight hundred Malay troops, and, under secret agreement with Meer Jaffir, threatened to dispossess the English of their privileges of trade, etc., Clive called out the Militia, a body of about three hundred, of whom nearly two hundred and fifty were Europeans; and a body of Volunteers was formed from amongst the respectable class of English, of whom about twenty or thirty formed a troop of horse, and about as many more an independent company of foot, who were available for any service."

At the battle of Bedarrah, near Chandernagore, when the English gained a decisive victory over the Dutch troops, while fifteen hundred of the nawab's cavalry looked on, but took no part in the engagement, "the troop of horse were very useful in pursuing the enemy."

Again, in 1763, when the English marched to Murshedabad, to depose Kossim Ali, the nawab of their own creating, the Militia were once more called out, and a company of Volunteers formed, "which company subsequently left Calcutta in charge of a fleet of store-boats, and continued to perform that duty till the close of the operations."

With the passing away of the days of struggle and stress, went the need for the Militia. The last body raised became the "Alipore Regiment" of Native Infantry, and was incorporated with the regular army. When, in the troubles of 1857, Volunteer troops once more paraded for service, they had the wide *maidan* for their parade-ground, and it is difficult now to realize what Calcutta must have been when that grassy plain was a jungle-grown swamp, and the only available parade-ground was the narrow strip beside the Great Tank.

A view of the east side of the Great Tank, painted in 1784, shows a narrow portion of the Parade Ground, on which are seen the figures of three Militia men, advancing in single file, musket on shoulder, dressed in a quaint uniform. A close-fitting coat of cut-away pattern shows a tight under-jacket, and broad belt, below which appears a garment, in the nature of a Highlander's trews. No draping kilt nor plaided stockings detract from its severe simplicity, which leaves the limbs to untrammelled freedom. The feet are unshod, and the head crowned with a conical hat apparently of matting.

All the details of this picture repay close study, the crowding figures at the Ghaut, ascending and descending the steep steps, the water carrier toiling under the heavy load of the full water-bag, the bent figure of age, led by a little child, the passing crowds in the street beyond, and over their heads the ungainly shapes of huge vultures flapping heavily through the air, or ranged in rows on the balustraded housetops.

In all the old views of Calcutta the street scenes are most striking, and in those executed by the Brothers Daniell the details are worked in with painstaking care, and repay close study.

THE GREAT TANK, 1788.

[*Face p.* 206.

In one, elephants are seen shuffling along, each followed by two or three spearmen, ready to goad the monster into submission should he get beyond the control of his driver, the *mahaut*, seated astride of his neck. In another a camel rears his uncouth head above the passers-by. Pack-bullocks share the roadway with four-horsed coaches, palanquins, sedans, and the native bullock-carriage. Dignified figures, in flowing robes, pace leisurely, under the shade of large mat umbrellas; while half-naked porters hurry along, carrying their loads slung on either end of a stout yet pliant bamboo, the *banghy*, laid across one shoulder. Beggars crouch in the wayside dust; a pariah dog slinks by; kites and crows hover above, and great adjutant birds —the *Argala*, bone-swallower—stand apart from the traffic, in sedate and watchful groups.

Many a ghastly tragedy was enacted in these same streets, along which haggard penitents passed, measuring with their own outstretched length every foot of the way to Kali's shrine; and ash-bedaubed *jogies*, religious mendicants, insolently proud of their degraded hideousness, demanded gifts in the name of alms, and cursed with horrid imprecation any who incurred their displeasure. When cholera swept the town, the dead lay on the roadside, where they were thrown in terror by those who should have performed the last rites; and in years of famine, when the famished villagers of the surrounding country-side sought the town in hope of succour, only to fall exhausted in the unfamiliar streets, the dead and dying lay where they fell, a common prey to ravening bird and beast. It was in the public street, too, that the criminal met his death upon the scaffold. Executions, for robbery as well as murder, were in some cases carried out on or near the scene of the crime. Otherwise they took place at the cross-roads where Chitpore Road and Bentinck Street meet Bow Bazar; and it was here that a European soldier, named Gale, was hung for murder, in December, 1797.

It was in the same year, 1797, that an extraordinary and exciting scene took place in Sudder Street, just off Chowringhee Road, in a house which is now included in the buildings of the Imperial Museum. This house was the property of Mr. Peter Speke, member of Council, who built it in 1790. The grounds extended to Kyd Street, and included the Kyd Street Tank, a sheet of water which may be readily found marked on the "Plan of Calcutta, 1742." The public had the right of access to this tank, which Mr. Speke desired to keep private, and to surround with a garden; to obtain which purpose an ingenious scheme was devised. The *ghaut* was removed from the east bank, to the south side, where the boundary was formed by the then new road, Kyd Street, named after General Alexander Kyd, who built and lived in the house which has been for so many years the United Service Club. The ghaut opened on this road, and over the steps an arch was thrown, and was built up with a perforated wall, which, while it allowed the water to flow freely through, effectually shut out the people who came to draw water from entering the tank, which was surrounded by a high wall. It was this perforated wall which obtained for the tank its native name of Jhinjherrie Talao (the "Mesh-work Tank").

In May, 1797, Mr. Speke had refused to receive a petition from a young Sikh, who, becoming importunate, was turned out of the house. Resenting this treatment, the unfortunate man, rushing into the house, killed two servants, and tried to enter Mr. Speke's room. His bearer with great presence of mind locked his master's door and misled the murderer, who, ascending the wrong staircase, reached the terraced roof, and was trapped. A party of sepoys—after trying in vain for some hours to reach the roof, the murderer keeping them at bay by pulling up the balustrades, and throwing the masonry on them in the narrow passage—broke loopholes in the wall of the staircase, and shot him dead, in the sight of an immense crowd gathered below.

The house was afterwards rented to Government by Mr. Speke for the Sudder Dewanny Court, and led to the name of the street being changed from Speke Road to Sudder Street, a name which it bears to this day.

The custom of naming streets after the most important resident has perpetuated the memory of Sir Henry Russell, a former Chief Justice; of Sir John Royds, a judge of the Supreme Court, who lived in the house afterwards the Doveton College; and of Lieutenant Camac, an Engineer officer, who, when the town was spreading southward, took up land in a hitherto unbuilt locality, and erected dwelling-houses as a speculation—as did Colonel Wood, another Engineer officer, on an adjoining piece of land.

Park Street, as all Calcutta residents are aware, received its name at a time when the more sensitive ears of a later generation were offended by the blunt "Burying Ground Road" of their predecessors. The "Park" was formed by the extensive grounds of a house in which

Sir Elijah Impey resided, on a site in Middleton Row, now occupied by Lorretto House, the Roman Catholic convent. In front of the old house was a circular pond, or tank, at the exact spot where Middleton Row turns at right angles, and the present road runs over what was the carriage-drive from Park Street to the house. That a large house, probably the identical house of Sir Elijah Impey's time, stood on this spot, surrounded by the same grounds, nearly half a century before his day, may be seen by reference to the "Plan of Calcutta" of 1742: it cannot have been an English residence, and was possibly the property of a native official. When Middleton Street was made about 1815, and named after Bishop Middleton, the first Bishop of Calcutta, then newly created a Bishopric, the old house was still standing, but within a few years it was "improved" away, and Middleton Row cut up the old Park, and afforded eligible building sites for speculative builders.

Opening into Park Street nearly opposite to Middleton Row is Free School Street, leading to the Free School. This school was established in 1790, in connection with the Mission Church, and in 1800 it was united to the old Charity School, then seventy-one years old. About the time that the two schools were united, a house in Jaun Bazaar, in which Justice Lemaistre, one of the judges who tried Nuncomar, had lived, was purchased for their accommodation, and there they have remained ever since. The present spacious buildings, however, present a very different appearance to the old house, which fell in 1854, through jackals undermining the foundations. When the school first moved into the Jaun Bazar house, the lands surrounding it were mostly open fields among which were scattered villages, with here and there a garden house, standing in wide grounds. The road leading to it from Jaun Bazar was called Jaun Bazar Fourth Lane, and another lane led to Park Street. It was on the line of these two lanes that Free School Street was made, about 1810.

One street, not usually connected with a personal name, is Swallow Lane, where lived, at the time the streets were being named, one Mr. L'Hirondelle; another street, generally supposed, mistakenly, to have received the name of a resident, is Cotton Street, which was known, long before it obtained the English appellation, as *Rooie-Hutta*, or Cotton Market, where, on the highest ground in all Calcutta, raw cotton used to be sold, in all probability to the spinners and weavers of old Chuttanutty.

Another name dating from the earliest years of the English settlement remains in Boitakhana, the locality at the Circular Road end of Bow Bazar. The tree which marked the *Boitakhana*, or Meeting-place — literally "Sitting-place,"— does not appear to have been an old tree, though it was, no doubt, large and shady. It stood on the edge of the Mahratta Ditch, just opposite the Avenue, as Bow Bazar was called, and must have commanded a clear view of the old Fort, to the main gate of which this wide road led. In 1799, when the Mahratta Ditch was filled up, and the road which followed its course on the town side was widened, and became the present Circular Road, the Boitakhana tree which stood right in the course of the new road was cut down. The felling of the tree caused some little stir at the time, as it was said to be an object of veneration to the natives. The circumstance was reported to the Governor-General, Lord Mornington, who desired that the tree should be spared, but found that it had already been cut down. On inquiry, it was found that the supposed veneration arose from the fact that Suraj-ud-Dowlah, when directing the siege of Fort William, had sat under this tree, safely out of the reach of danger.

CHAPTER X

NEAR AND FAR

Hughly—The Portuguese—Introduction of tobacco—Chinsurah—Serampore—The Serampore missionaries—River scenes—*Suttie*—Barrackpore—Dum Dum.

WHEN the English arrived in Bengal, in the seventeenth century, they first settled in Hughly, in the year 1633, nearly sixty years before Calcutta was founded. The Portuguese, who were the earliest European traders in India in modern times, had been in Bengal a hundred years before the English, and it was they who founded the town of Hughly, on the bank of the new course of the Ganges. In process of time the new town drew away the trade of the ancient city of Satgaon, which, deserted by the main stream of the river, was growing yearly more difficult of access for merchant vessels, as the old bed of the stream silted up more and more; and the Portuguese grew rich and powerful, and made their influence felt throughout the land.

It is said that it was in the early years of

their settlement at Hughly that the Portuguese introduced tobacco to the notice of the Emperor Akbar, and that the Indian pipe, the *hookah*, was invented. Mr. H. G. Keene, in his delightful "Handbook to Agra," has quoted an account of life at the court of Akbar, from an imaginative sketch by Mr. J. W. Sherer, C.S.I., which was published in 1852, from which the following extract regarding the introduction of tobacco may be taken. The emperor is supposed to have noticed during the day two Portuguese priests standing amongst the crowd to see him pass by, and to have commanded their attendance in the evening, when the emperor being seated surrounded by his courtiers, the priests also being present,—

"conversation was going on in desultory way, when the younger priest remarked that he had something very singular to show the emperor, if it was his pleasure to see it. Curiosity was excited; Akbar said certainly, that he wished to see everything novel and rare, and begged the priest to exhibit. The young man, feeling in a pocket under his cassock, said that he required a light. This was immediately ordered, and then he, retiring a little, applied the fire to something which he held concealed in his hand, after which smoke was seen issuing out of his mouth.

"At this Akbar laughed contemptuously, and

said that every juggler in the country that frequented fairs would do it ten times better. 'Why,' he cried, 'they will bring fire out of their nostrils, as well as smoke! If your magic was no better than this, you would not make one rupee a month.'

"This badinage was put an end to by the young priest explaining that there was no feat intended in producing the smoke, but that the curiosity was that the smoke itself was very soothing and agreeable, and that from partaking of it the mind of man became philosophic and cheerful. The priest then opened his hand, showed a small clay pipe, he also exhibited some of the fragrant weed from out of his pouch. Akbar was much interested, and sent immediately for Hukim Abul Futteh Gilani, to ask his opinion of the herb. He insisted, in the mean time, on trying it, much against the remonstrances of Abdul Kadir, who was now present, and assured him it was a device of the devil, and had probably been brought direct from his Satanic Majesty by his servants and emissaries the priests. When the hukim came, he found the emperor coughing very much; for Akbar, not being quite up to the mysteries of the pipe, had swallowed a good deal of smoke, and was suffering accordingly. The hukim with a grave face examined the herb, and afterwards, being ordered by the emperor to try it, declared that it was a pleasant and, possibly, a heathful weed, but that the smoke required purifying before it was imbibed. 'What is it called?' asked Akbar. 'Tobacco,' answered the priest. Akbar agreed with the hukim, that the smoke would be better for purification, but inquired how this could be better effected. The hukim replied that he thought it might be made to pass through water, and from that night he commenced the series of experiments which ended in the invention of the hukah."

The Portuguese traders in Bengal were favoured by the tolerant Akbar, and retained their privileges under his son and successor, Jehangir; Hughly continued to grow in importance and wealth, and the merchants grew proportionately more arrogant and proud. They domineered over the Mohammedan governors of Satgaon; having acquired land on both banks of the river, they exacted duties from all vessels passing up and down the great waterway, and raided the country-side for slaves, who were sent to their possessions in Southern India and elsewhere. In 1632 the Emperor Shah Jehan, having newly succeeded to the throne of Delhi, gave orders that the "European idolaters," the Roman Catholic Portuguese, were to be expelled from his kingdom. Hughly was accordingly attacked by a Mogul army, and, after a stubborn defence of over three months, was betrayed by a Portuguese half-caste, named De Mello, and the Portuguese power utterly destroyed. In Stewart's history it is stated that—

"when Hughly was destroyed, in A.D. 1632, by order of the Emperor Shah Jehan, there were sixty-four large vessels, fifty-seven grabs, and two hundred sloops anchored opposite the town, of which only one grab and two sloops escaped. The captain of the largest vessel, on which were embarked two thousand men, women, and children, with all their wealth, rather than yield to the Mohammedans, set fire to the magazine, and blew them up. Many other ships followed his example. Hughly, having came into possession of the Moguls, was established as the royal fort of Bengal. All the public offices were withdrawn from Satgaon, which soon declined into a mean village, now scarcely known to Europeans."

When the Portuguese monopoly of the foreign trade of Bengal was thus destroyed, the English made an effort to take their place, but were unsuccessful till some years later, in 1640. In that year a daughter of the emperor was severely burned by her dress catching fire. Dr. Gabriel Boughton, one of the Company's surgeons at Surat, attended the princess at the emperor's desire, and restored her to health. He patriotically asked as his reward privileges of trade for his honourable masters; these were readily granted by the grateful monarch, and, shortly after, an English factory was allowed to be established in Hughly. The position of the English settlement in the centre of a large Mohammedan town led to constant friction, and, in the end, the Hughly factory became untenable, the English left Bengal and went away to Madras, and when they finally returned it was to Chuttanutty, where they founded Calcutta.

It was while the English were at Hughly that the French and Danes established themselves in Bengal, about the year 1676. Taking warning from the difficulties experienced by the English, they obtained land on which to build their factories at some distance from Hughly and from each other, but on the river for the convenience of shipping their goods. The Dutch who arrived in Hughly during the Portuguese times had also a factory, but they selected a spot adjoining Hughly, and, in their plodding, phlegmatic way, kept themselves to themselves, and prospered accordingly. Captain Hamilton thus described their factory in the early years of the eighteenth century:—

"About half a league further up is Chinsurah, where the Dutch emporium stands. It is a large factory, walled high with brick. And the factors have a great many good houses standing pleasantly on the river's side; and all of them have pretty gardens to their houses. The settlement at Chinsurah is wholly under the Dutch Company's Government. It is about a mile long, and about the same breadth, well inhabited by Armenians and the natives. It is contiguous to Hughly, and affords sanctuary for many poor natives, when they are in danger of being oppressed by the mogul's governor or his harpies."

Chinsurah was given up to the English about the year 1825, when the Dutch received in exchange the British possessions in Sumatra. Some five years later the Government pulled down the old Dutch Government House, and the fort, Fort Gustavus, to make way for ranges of barracks, which were later abandoned as unsuitable. The old fort bore the date 1687 on its northern gate, and 1692 on the south gate, and contained in its structure some immense beams of Java teak, which had been brought up from Batavia, and which "were found to be as sound as the day they were inserted into the building."

According to a writer in the *Calcutta Review* of sixty years ago,[1] the church at Chinsurah—

[1] No. VIII., vol. iv., Dec., 1845.

THE HUGHLY IMAMBARA.

QUADRANGLE OF IMAMBARA.

[*Face p.* 221.

"was the joint gift of Mr. Sichterman and Mr. Vernet. Sichterman erected the steeple with a chime clock in 1744, and Vernet added the church twenty-four years afterwards; thus reminding us of the popular remark, that the Frenchman invented the frill, and the Englishman added the shirt."

Another church at Chinsurah was that of the Armenians, which still stands. It was built in 1695, by "Coja Johannes, the son of Marcar," who, according to his epitaph in the church, "was a great merchant, honoured with the favour of kings and viceroys. He travelled north, south, east, and west, and died at Hughly, in Hindustan, 7th November, 1697."

There are two other buildings of note, the Hughly College and the Imambara. The college is located at Chinsurah, in a large house which was built, in the eighteenth century, by a Frenchman who had acquired a handsome fortune in the military service of the Mahrattas. The Imambara is at Hughly, and was erected and endowed, as was the college, from a fund established by a Mohammedan gentleman, Mahommed Moshin, for the purpose of erecting an institution of public instruction, and a place of Mohammedan worship which should also be a centre of learning.

Bandel, which lies immediately above Hughly,

was a religious settlement of the Portuguese, founded by Augustinian friars from Goa. The Bandel church is the oldest building for Christian worship in Bengal; it was built in 1660, and contains the keystone of an earlier church, dated 1599, which was destroyed when Hughly was taken by the Mohammedans.

The French, when they arrived in Bengal, built their factory a few miles further down the river than Chinsurah, at Chandernagore, which, after many vicissitudes, is still French territory at the present day. Captain Hamilton, the free-spoken old trader, wrote severely of the French at Chandernagore, who,—

"for want of money, are not in a capacity to trade. They have a few private families dwelling near the factory, and a pretty little church to hear mass in, which is the chief business of the French in Bengal."

The matter-of-fact captain visited Chandernagore about 1720; by 1740 the town had been transformed under the energetic rule of Dupleix; and when, in 1742, the European traders were allowed, in consideration of the turbulent state of the country, to fortify their settlements, the French built an imposing fort, which they called Fort Orleans, and which was much stronger than the English fort in Calcutta. When Fort Orleans fell, in 1757, to Clive and Admiral Watson, the prosperity of the factory passed away; nor did it ever revive, for from that date the English became more powerful every year, and one by one their rivals, in trade and politics alike, withdrew, leaving them in sole possession of the country, which for centuries had been one great battlefield, on which foreign invaders fought and struggled for dominion over the fair land which they laid waste.

While France still clings to her bright little settlement in Bengal, the Danes at Serampore, like the Dutch at Chinsurah, realized that their Indian possessions had become useless to them, and, in 1845, the King of Denmark transferred his Indian settlements to the British Government, receiving in return a sum of twelve lacs of rupees; and now, beyond the Danish royal monogram on the church and on the gateway of the magistrate's house, and a few names on the old tombstones in the cemetery, nothing remains in Serampore to tell of the Danish occupation.

The Serampore church, strangely enough, was never occupied by a Danish minister. It was built in 1805 by public subscription, to which Lord Wellesley contributed a thousand rupees, on the ground, it was said, that a church steeple would crown the beauty of the distant view of Serampore, as seen from the Governor-General's country seat at Barrackpore, on the opposite shore of the Hughly river. The church had not long been completed when the town passed into the hands of the English. Although in Bengal the representatives of the two nations were on friendly terms, the outbreak of hostilities in Europe obliged them to adopt a similar course. On intelligence arriving in Calcutta of war having been declared between England and Denmark, a detachment of troops from Fort William took possession of Serampore, at six o'clock on the morning of the 28th of January, 1808; at the same time, a naval detachment seized the Danish ships lying in the river off the town. With that event the trade of the settlement ceased, and when, in 1815, the town was restored to the Danish Crown, but few Danes remained as residents.

During the seven years of the English occupation, the church was in the charge of the Baptist missionaries, and they continued to conduct services in it till, in 1845, the town came finally under the English Government, when the church was transferred to the care of a chaplain. It is the "Serampore missionaries" who have given the town its chief interest, and claim to notice.

Dr. Carey, the pioneer of the band, arrived in India in 1793. Finding that the allowance of fifty rupees a month, which it was arranged that he should receive from the newly formed Baptist Missionary Society in England, was totally inadequate for the support of himself and his family, he accepted the offer of Mr. Udny, at Malda, to take charge of an indigo factory at Mudnabatty, on a salary of two hundred rupees a month. Carey remained at Malda for over five years, combining indigo-planting with missionary work, the study of Sanskrit and Bengallee, and the translation of the Scriptures.

In 1799 four other Baptist missionaries arrived, to support Carey and his associate, Mr. Thomas, a ship's surgeon, whose early missionary efforts had in the first instance turned the Society's thoughts to India as a mission-field. Of the four new arrivals, one died within three weeks of landing, and another twenty months later; Thomas also died, and the three survivors—Carey, Marshman, and Ward—remained to carry on, for over thirty years, the enterprise which they then began with so much zeal, and to leave a remarkable record of accomplished work, with which their names are inseparably associated.

The four missionaries journeyed to India in 1799 in an American ship, no doubt for reasons of economy. Being without friends in Calcutta to receive them, they, on their captain's advice, proceeded up the river by boat, and found quarters at Serampore, where they were made welcome by the Danish officials. An amusing printer's error in a Calcutta newspaper led to their remaining at Serampore for the rest of their lives. Their arrival was announced in the paper as that of four Papist, instead of Baptist, missionaries, and, as there was much talk at the time of French spies entering the country in the guise of priests, the notice attracted the attention of the Calcutta Government, and placed the new-comers under suspicion, which left a feeling of distrust long after the mistake had been explained. The occurrence decided the missionaries to remain at Serampore; there Carey joined them, and there the devoted band laboured, as their memorial in the church records, "to the end of their lives, in the cause of religion and humanity."

Before leaving the old settlements and factories on the right bank of the Hughly, it may be well to pause, and recall something of the appearance the river must have presented to the dwellers on its shores, and some of the scenes that were enacted on its banks.

Up to the time when, in the latter half of the nineteenth century, railways began to ramify

CARGO BOATS ON THE HUGHLY.

CHANDERNAGORE FROM THE RIVER.

[*Face p.* 227.

through the country, the Ganges and its numerous branches were the great highways of commerce, and were crowded with an endless variety of craft. The European nations who traded in Bengal all sailed their ships up the Hughly, whether for merchandise or war, and when in times of peace the respective Governors of the settlements exchanged visits, and enjoyed each others hospitality, they travelled in their grand state barges, with a flotilla of lesser boats bearing their suite and attendants.

Stavorinus, the Dutch traveller of the eighteenth century, described in detail the visit of the Dutch "Director" of Chinsurah to the Governor of Calcutta in 1770. The Dutchman sailed in his great "budgerow," or house-boat, in the large room of which thirty-six people could sit down to table. He was followed by a crowd of smaller budgerows, with his officers; there were two kitchen, or "cook-boats," and two store-boats laden with the necessary provisions; making a fleet of thirty-three vessels, which sailed from Chinsurah, at four o'clock one afternoon, and arrived at Chitpore, the northern extreme of Calcutta, at seven next morning. After a stay of two days, which cost the Director a thousand rupees in *buckseesh* to the Governor's servants, the fleet sailed again with the flood tide, and proceeded up the river to Chandernagore, and so back to Chinsurah.

The Governors of Calcutta were by no means behind hand with their state boats, and, up to the introduction of steamers and railways, the Governor-General's "yacht" was his chief if not sole means of visiting distant provinces. When Lord Wellesley, in 1801, made a tour in the "Upper Provinces" his journey occupied eight months, although it extended no further than Lucknow and Cawnpore. For a week-end visit to his country seat at Barrackpore, the Governor would use his state barge; and Lord Valentia recorded his admiration of the animated aspect of the river there, at the time of his visit in 1803. "The state barges and cutters of the Governor-General, painted green and ornamented with gold, contrasted with the scarlet dresses of the rowers, were a great addition to the scene."

The tales of travellers, and the sober columns of the *Calcutta Gazette*, which tell of all this brave pomp and show, record also grim details of tragedies the most moving. The river waves, which bore these proud galleys, washed over the stiffening limbs of the dying, gasping out their latest breath on the muddy banks. And when the last breath had fled, they tossed the worn bodies to and fro in their ebb and flow, carrying disease and death through all the land. Down in the lower reaches, where the great river rushes to the sea, frenzied devotees cast their helpless children, or flung themselves amid the swirling waters where the hungry jaws of alligators waited to devour them. And everywhere, up and down the hundreds of miles of the mighty river's course, on its banks were reared the ghastly funeral pyres, on which the living and the dead were consumed together in the awful rite of *suttie.*

Every one has heard of the inhuman custom of *suttie*, but few can realize what the terrible reality meant. The following account, taken from the *Calcutta Gazette* of 10th February, 1785, presents a vivid picture, all the more striking for the plain matter-of-fact language in which it is couched :—

" An Account of a Woman burning herself. (By an Officer.)—A few days since, going in a budgerow from Ghyretty to dine at Chinsurah, I perceived near Chandernagore a vast crowd assembled on the shore; upon inquiry, I found this large concourse of people were gathered to see a Gentoo[1] woman burn herself with her husband. As I had read many accounts of this

[1] Hindoo.

strange and barbarous ceremony, but had never seen it performed, I was resolved upon the present occasion to be an eye-witness. I went ashore, and walked up close to the girl; she seemed about twenty-one years of age, and was standing up, decorated with flowers; pieces of silk were tied upon her wrists. Two of her children were near her; the eldest, about eight or nine years of age, was mixing up rice in a large pan, some of which, with many ceremonies, he put into his deceased father's mouth, who was laid upon his back on the pile: this was composed of straw and dry wood, and about four feet high; close round it were six bamboo stakes drove into the ground, about seven feet in height, to keep the pile from giving way too soon after the fire was communicated to it. The girl to me appeared stupid, and so very weak, that two Brahmins were obliged to support her. I asked some persons present whether bhang or opium had not been given to her; they declared not, but that the loss of her husband was the sole cause of her dejection. I however perceived, from the redness of her eyes, that narcotics had been administered; she seemed not in the least ruffled, but surveyed the crowd with great composure, nor did the dreadful preparations appear in the smallest degree to disconcert her. The Brahmins took her down to the Ganges; she sat on the edge of the water and was bathed, while prayers were repeated.

Her clothes were then taken off, and a red silk covering (a *saurry*) put upon her. When she returned from the river, fresh flowers were again put round her neck and arms. At this time, the Brahmins alone asked her, whether the sacrifice she was about to make of herself was her own free choice; and whether any force had been used to compel her to devote herself to death contrary to her inclination. She bowed her head, but I could not hear anything she said, or perceive that she spoke at all. She afterwards sat down, and threw several handfuls of cowries among the crowd, which were scrambled for with great avidity. She then took leave of her children and relations in a very affecting manner. The Brahmins afterwards fixed several combs in her hair, and led her six or seven times round her husband's corpse. I perceived, as often as she came to his head she bowed, and some words were repeated by those who attended her which I could not understand; she then was lifted upon the pile, and laid herself down by her deceased husband, with her arms about his neck. Two people immediately passed a rope twice across the bodies, and fastened it so tight to the stakes that it would have effectually prevented her from rising had she attempted. I could not refrain, at this moment, from asking a person who had been near me all the time, and who had been very ready in explaining every circumstance I had wished to be informed of, the reason of their binding down with cords a willing victim; he told me that, however great her resolution might be, it was very possible, when the fire was first kindled, she might attempt to rise, which the ropes would hinder her from doing. A great quantity of straw and dry wood was now laid upon her, and several pots of ghee thrown over it. The preparations, after the unhappy creature was laid upon the pile, took up some time, and this dreadful interval must have appeared to her more terrible than the worst of deaths. She distinctly heard the people around her ordering more fuel, and the fatal brand called for which was to consume her to ashes. When everything was ready, her eldest son came and set fire to the under part of the straw: in a moment all was in a blaze. Two men kept a very long bamboo closely pressed upon the bodies, but the heat was so great that people were constantly employed for some time pouring pots of water upon their heads. Vast quantities of straw, wood, etc., were thrown upon the pile for several minutes after it was lighted, and the heat was so great, that a termination must have been very soon put to the torments of the miserable devoted woman."

The practice of *suttie* was abolished by Lord William Bentinck in 1829, when it was made a criminal act, punishable by death, to assist a woman in self-destruction.

On the left bank of the Hughly, opposite to Serampore, is Barrackpore, which takes its name from the barracks of the British troops stationed there. The country seat of the Viceroy is at Barrackpore, and affords a cool and restful retreat from the crowded town. Before Lord Wellesley's time the Governors did not make a practice of leaving Calcutta for the country, though Warren Hastings used to take his wife up the river to Rishera, just below Serampore, where they had a residence, Rishera House.

When Lord Wellesley established the Governor's country residence at Barrackpore, he took over the bungalow from the Commander-in-Chief, to whom he paid an allowance of five hundred rupees a month to find himself a suitable house. The writer of an article on "The Left Bank of the Hughly," in the *Calcutta Review* for June, 1845, stated that Lord Wellesley proposed to build a "palace" in Barrackpore Park, at a cost of three or four lacs of rupees, and to remove all the public offices from Calcutta to Barrackpore. The Court of Directors, however, vetoed the scheme, which would have made modern Calcutta a very different city to what it is at the present day. The foundations of the "palace," which had been laid, were utilized, many years afterwards, by Lady Hastings for a greenhouse. The

Marquis of Hastings replaced the "temporary bungalow" which Lord Wellesley had built by a handsome and suitable mansion, and Barrackpore became the country residence of the Governors-General during the hot-weather months, at a time when "the Hills" were still unknown. At the present day, Government House, Barrackpore, is, what it has been for many years past, a week-end retreat for the Viceroy during the four months which he spends in Calcutta every year.

Just below Barrackpore Park a group of twenty-four small Hindu temples, clustered together, form an imposing and picturesque object on the bank, as seen from the river. These, the Tittaghur temples, are of comparatively recent date, having been built by a wealthy Hindu family about the close of the eighteenth century. They mark, however, a locality which for long years before that period had an evil reputation as the headquarters of a family of *Thugs*, or *phanseegars*—the stranglers. The *Thugs* were a caste of hereditary robbers who infested the highways of India, not only robbing their victims, but strangling them by means of a handkerchief fastened in a running noose. It was not till the nineteenth century was well advanced that these murderous highwaymen were effectually dealt with, when Colonel Sleeman, in charge of a

GOVERNMENT HOUSE, BARRACKPORE.

BARRACKPORE PARK.

[*Face p.* 234.

special department of police, hunted them down, and, breaking up their gangs, relieved the country of their baneful presence on the highways.

Another military station in the neighbourhood of Calcutta is Dum Dum, lying away from the river, about four miles to the north-east of the town. In the old days, before the country had been drained, the Great Salt Water Lake, which lies to the east of Calcutta, ran up as far as Dum Dum. At that time the jungle-grown shores of the lake were the haunt of tigers and other wild beasts, and its waters of duck, and teal, and innumerable birds. Now it is a wide, treeless stretch of low-lying level land, the clay soil dry and cracked in the winter months, but flooded in the rainy season, when it springs into verdure, and for mile upon mile the rice crop of the villages waves green. Just beyond this low land lies Dum Dum, and Dum Dum House, a well-built house, standing on a low artificial hill, or rather mound, once surrounded by a moat, portions of which still remain. The late Mr. R. C. Sterndale, who once occupied Dum Dum House, had a theory that the mound had been thrown up and fortified in very ancient times, and that later it had been a stronghold of robbers, who, passing through the Salt Water Lake in their long and narrow swift-rowing boats, plundered inland villages, or, gaining the river, would attack the slow-moving heavy cargo boats and merchant vessels, robbing and slaying with impunity, and carrying home their plunder to be hoarded away in subterranean chambers and passages.

Whatever may have been the early history of the spot, it was in the days of Clive's Government, between 1757 and 1767, that Dum Dum House was built, for the benefit of change of air for the convalescent servants of the Company, after illness. A similar sanitarium was established at Baraset, but the bungalows erected there were less substantial than the house at Dum Dum. They were converted later into quarters for the young cadets of the Bengal establishment on their arrival in the country, and when the system was altered the cadet establishment at Baraset was done away with, and the connection with the military ceased, leaving only a weed-grown cemetery as a mournful memorial of the past.

Dum Dum, from being a sanitarium, grew to a military camp. When Colonel Pearce's detachment of Artillery returned from Madras in 1785, they were quartered at Dum Dum Camp, and were there reviewed in February, 1786, by the Commander-in-Chief, on which occasion Colonel Pearce "gave an elegant entertainment, at which were present, besides the Commander-in-Chief and the Governor-General, a very numerous and respectable company."

Dum Dum is now a quiet and dull little station, with an undesirable reputation for damp and malaria. In its early years it was the scene of many brilliant entertainments, and the centre of much generous hospitality. As the station grew, it became the fashionable resort for Calcutta society, and many a gay cavalcade of fine ladies and gentlemen passed along the raised Dum Dum Road to be present at a grand review, or to grace a performance in the little theatre with their presence, and wind up with an elaborate supper, when toasts were honoured with "three times three." The gay dames and gallants have long slept quietly in their far-scattered tombs, but the memory of their bright passing to and fro lingers in the country-side, where the simple village folk, as they gazed after them across the level expanse of their rice-fields, threaded their own exclamations of pleasure at the sight on the melody of a song, which may yet be heard when, in the quiet evening hour, mothers croon their babes to rest :—

> "Dekho meri jan !
> Kampani nishan !
> Bibi gia Dum Dumma
> Oora hai nishan.

> Burra sahib, chota sahib,
> Banka Kapitan.
> Dekho meri jan !
> Lia hai nishan."

Which may be freely translated :—

> " See, oh ! life of mine !
> The Company's ensign !
> The lady to Dum Dum hath gone,
> Flieth the ensign.
> Great men, little men,
> Officers so fine.
> See, oh ! life of mine !
> Goeth the ensign."

Like the East India Company itself, and its servants before whom it fluttered, alike in the gay processions of peace as in the stern ranks of war, the Company's *nishan*, their badge and symbol of power, has passed away from the land. And, day by day, as the years go by, the memory of it fades, and "the old order changeth, yielding place to new."

BADGE OF THE EAST INDIA COMPANY

INDEX

INDEX

INDEX

INDEX

INDEX

INDEX

THE END